Pentecost 1

Aids for Interpreting
the Lessons of the Church Year

Pentecost 1

David A. Hubbard

Elizabeth Achtemeier, series editor

Series B

FORTRESS PRESS   Philadelphia

COPYRIGHT © 1985 BY FORTRESS PRESS

Second printing 1988

Library of Congress Cataloging in Publication Data
Main entry under title:

Proclamation 3.

Consists of 28 volumes in 3 series designated A, B,
and C which correspond to the cycles of the three year
lectionary. Each series contains 8 basic volumes with
the following titles: Advent-Christmas, Epiphany, Lent,
Holy Week, Easter, Pentecost 1, Pentecost 2, and
Pentecost 3.
1. Bible—Homiletical use.   2. Bible—Liturgical
lessons, English.   I. Achtemeier, Elizabeth Rice,
1926–
BS534.5.P765   1985   251   84–18756
ISBN 0–8006–4106–X (Series B, Pentecost 1)

3396K87   Printed in the United States of America   1–4106

Contents

Series Foreword

Proclamation 3 is an entirely new aid for preaching from the three-year ecumenical lectionary. In outward appearance this new series is similar to *Proclamation: Aids for Interpreting the Lessons of the Church Year* and *Proclamation 2*. But *Proclamation 3* has a new content as well as a new purpose.

First, there is only one author for each of the twenty-eight volumes of *Proclamation 3*. This means that each author handles both the exegesis and the exposition of the stated texts, thus eliminating the possibility of disparity between scholarly apprehension and homiletical application of the appointed lessons. While every effort was made in *Proclamation: Aids* and in *Proclamation 2* to avoid such disparity, it tended to creep in occasionally. *Proclamation 3* corrects that tendency.

Second, *Proclamation 3* is directed primarily at homiletical interpretation of the stated lessons. We have again assembled the finest biblical scholars and preachers available to write for the series; now, however, they bring their skills to us not primarily as exegetes, but as interpreters of the Word of God. Exegetical material is still presented—sometimes at length—but, most important, here it is also applied; the texts are interpreted and expounded homiletically for the church and society of our day. In this new series scholars become preachers. They no longer stand back from the biblical text and just discuss it objectively. They engage it—as the Word of God for the worshiping community. The reader therefore will not find here the divisions between "exegesis" and "homiletical interpretation" that were marked off in the two earlier series. In *Proclamation 3* the work of the pulpit is the context and goal of all that is written.

There is still some slight diversity between the several lections and calendars of the various denominations. In an effort to overcome such diversity, the North American Committee on a Common Lectionary issues an experimental "consensus lectionary" *(The Common Lectionary)*, which is now being tried out in some congregations and which will be further altered at the end of a three-year period. When

7

the final form of that lectionary appears, *Proclamation* will take account of it. In the meantime, *Proclamation 3* deals with those texts that year used by *most* denominations on any given Sunday. It also continues to use the Lutheran numbering of the Sundays "after Pentecost." But Episcopalians and Roman Catholics will find most of their stated propers dealt with under this numbering.

Each author writes on three lessons for each Sunday, but no one method of combining the appointed lessons has been imposed upon the writers. The texts are sometimes treated separately, sometimes together—according to the author's own understanding of the texts' relationships and messages. The authors interpret the appointed texts as these texts have spoken to them.

One of the leading evangelicals of our times, David Allan Hubbard is the President of Fuller Theological Seminary and Professor of Old Testament. He is the author of dozens of books and articles, an internationally known speaker, a prominent educator, and a distinguished scholar. Among his recent books are *Beyond Futility, The Practice of Prayer,* and *Right Living in a World Gone Wrong.*

The Day of Pentecost

Lutheran	Roman Catholic	Episcopal	Pres/UCC/Chr	Meth/COCU
Ezek. 37:1–14	Acts 2:1–11	Acts 2:1–11 or Isa. 44:1–8	Joel 2:28–32	Acts 2:1–21 or Ezek. 37:1–14
Acts 2:1–21	1 Cor. 12:3b–7, 12–13	1 Cor. 12:4–13 or Acts 2:1–11	Acts 2:1–13	1 Cor. 12:4–13
John 7:37–39a	John 20:19–23	John 20:19–23 or John 14:8–17	John 16:5–15	John 16:5–15

FIRST LESSON: EZEKIEL 37:1–14

Pentecost is about hope—hope prompted by the knowledge that the Spirit is at work in the midst of God's people. The prophet Ezekiel described that work in stark and graphic terms as nothing less than a resurrection of dry, disconnected bones. His account of the new life that the Spirit was to breathe into exiled Israel is one way in which the Old Testament blazes a trail for Pentecost.

The broad valley or plain (Ezek. 37:1–2) littered with bones depicts *the helpless condition of the people.* So stern was the judgment which their rebellion evoked that they had no hope of recovery on their own. Neither a new political organization nor a fresh spiritual commitment was within their power. They were dead.

The word "bone" underscores this. To the Hebrews bone was more than a compact cluster of calcium bracing the flesh. Bones were deeply affected by what happened to the person. Hezekiah (Isa. 38:13), Job (30:17), and the psalmists (6:2; 31:10, etc.) all complain about bones being weakened or broken by illness or persecution. Once bones are quoted as singing a hymn in praise of God's uniqueness—the word parallel to bones is soul (Ps. 35:9–10), as though bones were synonymous with self or person. Ezekiel's arid scene speaks of the total loss of vitality of God's people; the bones, the sensitive inner essence which, depending on circumstances, can ache or rejoice, are devoid of life.

9

God's question spotlights Israel's helplessness: "Can these bones live?" (Ezek. 37:3). So does Ezekiel's answer, "O Lord God, thou knowest." The whole valley smacked of death. Only God could know whether revival was possible, because only God could bring revival.

Next, the focus moves to *the boundless power of the Spirit,* the only answer adequate to the helplessness. The Spirit of power transported the prophet to the valley, enabling him to witness the plight of the exiled people (v. 1). The Spirit's power dominates the climax of the passage (v. 14) in the salvation promise: "I will put my Spirit within you, and you shall live."

In between, the need of the Spirit's power is pressed home by a triple prophecy announcing the restoration in stages: (1) God's first command is, "Prophesy to these bones" (v. 4), and, as a result, "The bones came together, bone to its bone" (v. 7) and sinews, flesh, and skin covered them; "but there was no breath in them" (v. 8); (2) the second command is, "Prophesy to the breath" (v. 9), and, as a result, "the breath came into them, and they lived" (v. 10); (3) the third command is, "Prophesy (to the whole house of Israel)," and the result is not stated but implied in the promises of opening graves, resurrecting the people, bringing them back to Israel (which had been prepared by the dramatic prophecy to the land in Ezek. 36:1–15), and placing God's Spirit within them (vv. 12–14).

Bones, sinew, flesh, and skin do not a human being make. Full life is not possible until God's Spirit indwells God's people. Thus the structure of Ezekiel's vision helps set the stage for Pentecost.

So does the language, especially the prophecy to the breath (vv. 9–10). Ezekiel did not choose the word *nešāmāh,* which would have clearly connected this vision with the creation account of Gen. 2:7, where the dusty human frame is sparked to life by divine breath. Instead, the prophet used *rûₐh* to imply that God's universal Spirit, summoned from the four winds, that is, the whole earth, was the only force capable of revivifying that helpless multitude of reassembled bones and flesh.

The vision's final emphasis demonstrates *the matchless knowledge of the Lord.* Restoration of the helpless and resettlement of them from Mesopotamia to the land of promise are majestic themes, but they are not God's deepest motivation for the Spirit's work. What God seeks most is that his lordship be displayed and recognized: "And you shall know that I am the Lord" (v. 6); "Then you shall know that I, the

Lord, have spoken, and I have done it" (v. 14). These formulas of recognition and proof encapsulate God's prime purpose in human history and our key role as God's creatures. When the drama of resurrection, revivification, and restoration has rolled to its triumphant climax, center stage belongs not to the people but to their glorious Lord.

Pentecost is about hope—hope that reaches to our helplessness, hope that draws upon the Spirit's power, hope that delights in knowing who is truly God. Ezekiel's broad valley of bones is a mountaintop of revelation for all who go there with him to watch the Spirit work.

SECOND LESSON: ACTS 2:1–21

The account of the first Christian Pentecost is both a unique event (Acts 2:1–13) and an authoritative interpretation (Acts 2:14–36). As such, it follows a familiar biblical pattern in which God acts in history and then provides a prophet to declare the meaning of those acts. God worked in the midst of Egypt and had Moses present to expound the significance; God used Assyria like a rented razor and unfolded the meaning through Isaiah (7:20). Not deed without word, leaving the people mystified as to its meaning, not word without deed, leaving them uncertain of its authenticity, but deed with word, word with deed—they are the means by which God usually made his presence known.

The marks of Pentecost as *a unique event* are apparent. First, God is present. The signs of his presence echo the reports of theophanies in the Old Testament: "The rush of a mighty wind" (v. 2) recalls Yahweh's answer to Job "out of the whirlwind" (Job 38:1) and the "tongues of fire" remind us of Moses' burning bush (Exod. 3:2). A psalmist combines the two elements:

Who makest the winds thy messengers,
fire and flame thy ministers. (Ps. 104:4)

Think what this meant to the huddled group of believers just ten days after Jesus had disappeared from their sight on the mount of ascension: the living God was yet present in fullness of power, ready to indwell his people who were to become his living temples (1 Cor. 6:19).

Second, Pentecost is unique in its means of universal communication. The One who baptized the believers with the Holy Spirit and fire (Luke 3:16) gave them power to speak in tongues that were intelligible

to the vast host of foreigners gathered in Jerusalem to celebrate
Pentecost, as the law prescribed (Deut. 16:16). The long list of
homelands—ranging from the mountains east of Mesopotamia to the
coasts of Asia Minor and from the shorelines of North Africa to Rome
itself (vv. 9–11)—shows not only how dispersed were the Jews and the
God-fearers who had left their gentile religions to worship the true and
living God but how universal the church was to become. Not a sect of
provincial Galileans but a fellowship that girdled the Roman world,
the people of the risen Lord were to become the great new fact of
human history. Small wonder that some misread the event as a drunk-
en spree (vv. 12–13). God's unique acts often carry mystery and
misunderstanding, just as when Eli mistook Hannah's desperate
prayer for the mumblings of an inebriate (1 Sam. 1:13–14).

This misunderstanding gave Peter opportunity for his *authoritative
interpretation* of the unique event. Not drunken babblings but Joel's
prophetic vision was responsible for the extraordinary behavior. What
God had committed himself to perform centuries earlier was now
taking place before their eyes, and Joel's prophecy was the key to
understanding this: (1) the prophecy was being *fulfilled*—"this is
what was spoken by the prophet Joel" (v. 16; cf. Joel 2:28–32); (2) the
prophetic office was being *expanded*, women and men, old and young,
even servants were being equipped to speak for God—not just the
handful of Amoses or Ezekiels whose words the Scripture preserves
(vv. 17–18); Moses' prayer-wish that all God's people would be
prophets had come to pass (Num. 11:29); (3) the cosmic scope of the
prophetic event was *demonstrated*, even the eternal heavens and the
dependable sun and moon would be affected (vv. 19–20); (4) the
prophetic mission of proclaiming salvation would be *achieved*, when
those from every tribe and nation who call "on the name of the Lord"
will know the fullness of his rescue (v. 21).

A unique event authoritatively interpreted—that is Luke's picture
of Pentecost: unique because it is one of the milestones in the march of
salvation, like the incarnation, the crucifixion, the resurrection, the
ascension; authoritative because it was anticipated by the inspired
prophet Joel and interpreted by the inspired apostle Peter, fully
backed by the other eleven (v. 14). The long-awaited "last days" (v. 17)
which Joel's vision had foreseen, which Ezekiel's picture of resurrection had intimated (37:1–14), had dawned.

All believers since that day, sometime around A.D. 30, have entered into that baptism (1 Cor. 12:13) and had their names written into the story of Pentecost with that first one hundred twenty (Acts 1:15) and the three thousand who joined their ranks immediately (Acts 2:41). Pentecost was set originally to celebrate the wheat harvest (Exod. 34:22; Deut. 16:9), and year after year the assemblies of God's people had burst forth with shouts of gratitude. If staple grain could evoke that response, what should be our celebration of the presence of the Spirit, the inauguration of the church, and the worldwide harvest of those who call him Lord?

GOSPEL: JOHN 7:37–39a

Jesus' strong announcement about water was appropriate to the Feast of Tabernacles (John 7:2). As the Fall harvest festival, it gave opportunity to express thanks for rain and for the produce of the earth. And for centuries Tabernacles had included, on the seventh day, a ceremony that brought water from the pool of Siloam to the Temple. Another part of the background for Jesus' invitation may well have been the episode in Num. 20:10–13 when the Israelites drank from the stream that gushed from Moses' rock. Comparisons and contrasts between Christ and Moses are frequent in John's Gospel (1:17; 3:14; 6:41–51).

Jesus' boldness is astounding. He makes it impossible for the crowds to ignore him by standing, shouting, and inviting attention to himself (v. 37). No longer could the holy day be a national occasion of commemoration and thanksgiving. It became a day of personal decision.

Personal because *the invitation is to Christ personally:* "Come to me and drink" (7:37). Nothing is said about institutions or rituals or regulations. Surrounded by all the accoutrements of Jewish religion, Jesus centers attention solely on who he is and what he will do.

The decision is personal also because *the invitation is addressed to any one who will heed it:* "If any one thirst, let him come" (v. 37). No other requirements are tagged on; no fine print complicates the contract. The splendid offer recorded in Isaiah is made specific and visible in Jesus:

Ho every one who thirsts,
  come to the waters;
and he who has no money
  come buy and eat! (Isa. 55:1)

The decision is personal because *the invitation holds promise for other persons as well:* out of the heart of the one who comes to Jesus "shall flow rivers of living water" (v. 38). The promise entails not blessing for the thirsty recipient alone but a free-flowing abundance that spreads refreshment, as a river turns everything green along its banks (Ps. 1:3).

In the persons of Jesus and the thirsty who come to him are fulfilled the Old Testament pictures of Jerusalem: "There is a river whose streams make glad the city of God (Ps. 46:4); and "On that day living waters shall flow out from Jerusalem" (Zech. 14:8). And in Jesus and his thirsty followers is anticipated the description of the Holy City with "the river of the water of life, bright as crystal, flowing from the throne of God and of the Lamb" (Rev. 22:1).

The Fourth Gospel permits no speculation about this water: "Now this he said about the Spirit" (v. 39). The passage points to Pentecost and the new era of spiritual satisfaction and spiritual harvest which that great event inaugurated. It was the crucified Christ, glorified by the selfless offering of himself in love and risen from the dead, who poured out the Spirit on the fledgling church (v. 39; Acts 2:32–33). What the Gospel event foresaw, the first Pentecost fulfilled.

The Holy Trinity
The First Sunday After Pentecost

Lutheran	Roman Catholic	Episcopal	Pres/UCC/Chr	Meth/COCU
Deut. 6:4–9	Deut. 4:32–34, 39–40	Exod. 3:1–6	Isa. 6:1–8	Deut. 4:32–34, 39–40
Rom. 8:14–17	Rom. 8:14–17	Rom. 8:12–17	Rom. 8:12–17	Rom. 8:12–17
John 3:1–17	Matt. 28:16–20	John 3:1–16	John 3:1–8	John 3:1–17

FIRST LESSON: DEUTERONOMY 6:4–9

To grasp the full impact of this startling announcement, we need to see how polytheism among the neighbors of ancient Israel tended to carve life into compartments. Each deity ruled a separate area of life, from the cycles of seasons to the welfare of crops and the health of persons. The Babylonian and Assyrian pantheons were so sharply divided into specific realms of responsibility that individuals needed an organizational chart to tell them whom to call in time of need. The Canaanite religion was only slightly less complex.

Against this background came the summons for Israel to give solemn attention in its assembly to what the Lord had to say. The attention was more than warranted. Few statements in the entire history of civilization have had such revolutionary and permanent impact.

The announcement begins with *the oneness the Lord reveals*. Whichever translation we follow (the Hebrew reads "Yahweh, our God; Yahweh, one," and can be translated three or four ways), we come out the same: The Lord is the only God with whom Israel *is* to deal and *needs* to deal.

The Baals of Canaan and the gods of Ammon or Edom were to be rejected. Both the Decalogue (Exod. 20:1–17; Deut. 5:6–21) and this command (usually called the *Shema*, Hebrew for "hear") insist on a practical, vital monotheism which does not stoop to argue against the existence of other gods but implies that they are too powerless to be reckoned with. It was not Anat or Dagon who rescued Israel from Egypt but the Lord. The covenant that followed that rescue tolerated no other gods.

The Lord was all Israel needed. He is creator of heaven and earth, God of patriarchs, Conqueror of Pharaoh, Judge at Sinai, Guide through the wilderness. All that the people want he can supply, from the law that delights their lives to the food that nourishes their bodies.

This revelation of the Lord's oneness leads inevitably to *the loyalty the Lord demands*. The indicative mood of the divine declaration instantly becomes imperative.

The loyalty is to be *intense*. The imperative form is the strongest in Hebrew, the same form that drives home the Ten Commandments with full authority: "You shall love the Lord" (v. 5). It is love with no reservations.

The loyalty is to be *appropriate*. Love is the only fitting response to what God has already done. The early chapters of Deuteronomy rehearse God's acts of deliverance, step by step, through the Exodus and wilderness experience to make the points (1) that "the Lord your God is a merciful God" (4:31); and (2) that "he loved your fathers . . . and brought you out of Egypt with his own presence" (4:37). What God had given, he had given in love; what he, appropriately, asked in return was nothing less than that same love. Fear (6:2), obedience (6:2), trust (Prov. 3:5), and knowledge of God (Hos. 6:6) are all appropriate replies to God's grace. Yet none but love captures so clearly the combination of loyal commitment to and grateful recognition of the Lord's covenant. It links us to the very nature of God (1 John 4:8) by drawing out our deepest, finest human response (1 Corinthians 13).

The loyalty is to be *total*: all our choices are made in light of it ("heart"); our very being is defined in terms of it ("soul"); all our energies are devoted to it ("might").

It also becomes the very environment of our households: it occupies our constant attention (v. 6), forms the curriculum for the instruction of our children, decides the topics for our daily conversation (v. 7), determines our outlook on life, and sets the tone of our homes (v. 9; the language of frontlets and phylacteries was probably intended to be metaphorical but for centuries has been taken literally by Jews as a badge of their devotion to this command).

One Lord there is, and that Lord is to be totally loved. That is as basic a summary of biblical faith as we can find. No wonder many of our Jewish neighbors recite it three times a day; no wonder Jesus isolated it as the first great commandment (Matt. 22:37–38); no wonder the apostles built it into their summaries of the faith (Eph. 4:6); no wonder the church has affirmed it in all the great creeds and made it the cornerstone of its doctrine of the Holy Trinity.

SECOND LESSON: ROMANS 8:14–17

The New Testament spends no energy speculating on the nature of the Trinity. Rather, the apostles fix attention on the Trinity's ministry in the life of believers and of the church. Here, the Spirit's role is stressed.

The Spirit's work *in support of the believers* is described in a chain of key phrases. Each adds clarity to what precedes it, and each fleshes out the theme of our participation in God's family ("sonship"), which is the chief point of the whole passage.

In a nutshell, the text says that the Spirit's presence is the badge of our relationship to God. The surest sign that we are part of God's people—the masculine "sons" may indicate the special status that God's new people enjoy, though such status is not restricted by gender (Gal. 3:28)—is that *we are being led by the Spirit* (v. 14). The present tense of the verb stresses the process involved, a process that Paul has previously pictured as living by the Spirit's guidance and values rather than by the passions and selfishness of human instinct ("flesh," vv. 12–13).

The Spirit has only the highest good of believers in view. For Paul, this motive stands in sharpest contrast with that of both the misguided Jewish teachers who lead their disciples into slavery to law and the ignorant pagan priests who entice their pupils into slavery to superstitions. What the Spirit has in store is our full adoption as children of the heavenly Father with all the privileges of the household, including the boldness of family members, not the cowering anxiety of slaves (v. 15).

The account of the Spirit's support builds to a double climax. First, *we are enabled to call God Father* (vv. 15–16). The verb means "to cry aloud or shout strongly," with the emphasis not on volume but on assurance; the Aramaic term "Abba" rings with the delight of a child's address to a daddy, and may hint of the unique privilege of prayer as a key mark of God's children (see Rom. 8:26–27).

Second, *we are entitled to share Christ's inheritance* of glory (v. 17) on the far side of suffering. Nothing shows more forcefully the power of the Spirit's work than the ability to take aliens, rebels, slaves, and plant them permanently in the household of God where they enjoy all the privileges of the chief Heir, who welcomes them with none of the grudging reluctance of the prodigal son's elder brother (Luke 15:25–32).

The Spirit's ministry goes on *in service to the work of the Father and the Son,* as well as in support of the believers. In classical Christian theology, equality in power, glory, and deity of the three persons of the Trinity is a given: Father, Son, and Spirit share eternally the essence and attributes of divinity. Yet, just as the Son comes to do the Father's bidding (John 5:19), so the Spirit is sent by the Father (John 14:16) and the Son (Acts 2:33) to fulfill the divine mission by forming, empowering, and preserving the church. To accomplish this mission, both Son and Spirit become servants, doing the Father's will.

Paul's intent is to describe the Spirit's work. Yet, the Spirit's aim is not to make us spiritists but to graft us into the Father's family where we share the tasks and the rewards of the Lord Christ.

GOSPEL: JOHN 3:1–17

We are, here, eavesdroppers on one of history's crucial conversations. A devout, curious, esteemed Jewish leader, Nicodemus, has come, apparently to understand more about what Jesus had been teaching. As we follow the flow of the dialogue, we shall note how the early attention is on the work of the Spirit but the climax centers in the mission of Christ, and we shall grasp even more clearly why Christians have joyfully confessed their faith in the one true and living God: Father, Son, and Holy Spirit.

The conversation begins with *Nicodemus's compliment* (v. 2): he recognizes that God is present with Jesus and has enabled him to perform signs (miracles that teach spiritual lessons; John 2:1–11, 23). Nicodemus comes not as adversary or spy but as honest inquirer.

This first interchange concludes with *Jesus' condition* (v. 3): No true experience of the kingdom is possible without a birth from above (probably a better translation than "born again," given all the subsequent conversation about the earthly and heavenly realities to which Jesus has access; vv. 12–13). Jesus' bluntness is typical of his speech in John. His signs were foretastes of God's kingdom, demonstrations of the age to come; but no one could experience God's glorious future without a total change of affection and allegiance, comparable to a fresh birth, a birth not dependent on human initiative but effected from above.

Nicodemus's conundrum was apparent: another birth was an impossibility for a grown person (v. 4). He had taken Jesus' bait and was hooked into a misunderstanding which Jesus deliberately used to prepare him for the next step. *Jesus' clarification* is introduced by the double Amen which intensified the importance of the statement (v. 5; F.F. Bruce's translation is apt, "In deed and in truth"; cf. also 3:3, 11): the birth from above is explained as a birth of water and Spirit. Cleansing from sin and new power from the Spirit seem to have been Jesus' point, which Nicodemus should have caught from Ezekiel's promise: "I will sprinkle clean water upon you, and you shall be clean from all your uncleannesses. . . . And I will put my Spirit within you" (36:25, 27).

This clarification is carried forward by an *illustration* (v. 6), reinforced with a *command* (v. 7), and clinched with an *analogy* (v. 8).

Common sense teaches that like bears like. All human flesh can produce is more human flesh. A truly spiritual existence can be mothered by God's Spirit alone. Only thus can flesh overcome its limitations and enter the new world of the Spirit.

This telling argument leads relentlessly to the command: "You (the plural in Greek includes all of us eavesdroppers—not only you the Jewish teacher but everybody, everywhere, in every time) must be born from above." (v. 7). Jesus' comparison of the wind's invisible blowing and the mystery of the Spirit's ways is based on the fact that wind and Spirit are the same word in both Hebrew $(r\hat{u}^ah)$ and Greek *(pneuma)*. The birth from above is beyond human managing, though the results in changed life and loyalty are readily apparent.

At this point we overhear *Nicodemus's final puzzled question:* How can this be? (v. 10). Jesus' new way of dealing with devotion to God fit none of his ancient categories. The gracious expert, who himself bore all the marks of a good teacher, is left speechless.

Jesus' monologue declares his authority to speak of the Spirit's work: he has personally witnessed it (as did his followers—note the "we," v. 11) and, indeed, is the only one to have bridged the gap between heaven and earth (3:12–13) and thus gained the right to be the official interpreter of the relationship between those realms.

As the monologue continues (vv. 14–15), Jesus not only argues for his authority but describes his mission. What Moses' serpent did in temporal, physical healing to the snake-bitten tribes of Israel (Num. 21:5–9), Jesus' exaltation on the cross—John regularly sees the cross with its display of love, its provision of forgiveness, and its sign of obedience to the Father as an act of incomparable glory (8:28; 12:23, 32, 34)—will do to bring a whole new quality of life to all who rest their hopes in him.

The final verses (vv. 16–17) seem to be the *Evangelist's meditations* on all this. If Jesus' teachings about the Spirit's power to make life new and his own fundamental part in that newness have been confusing, behind the whole activity looms the sacrificial love of God poured out for the whole world. And with the most radical of results: not death but eternal life, not condemnation but salvation (v. 17).

The boundless love of the Father, the willing death of the Son, the ready help of the Spirit all conspire to draw us to believe in the reality of the divine work and the divine personhood. With the full power of divine persuasion, the Holy Trinity calls us to that life-giving, kingdom-entering belief and, even more, gives us grace to answer that call.

The Second Sunday After Pentecost

Lutheran	Roman Catholic	Episcopal	Pres/UCC/Chr	Meth/COCU
Deut. 5:12–15	Deut. 5:12–15	Deut. 5:6–21	Deut. 5:12–15	Deut. 5:12–15
2 Cor. 4:5–12	2 Cor. 4:6–11	2 Cor. 4:5–12	2 Cor. 4:6–11	2 Cor. 4:5–12
Mark 2:23–28	Mark 2:23—3:6 or Mark 2:23–28	Mark 2:23–28	Mark 2:23—3:6	Mark 2:23—3:6

FIRST LESSON: DEUTERONOMY 5:12–15

The church calendar itself is a tribute to the tenacity of this command. The weeks that roll by from Advent to Lent to Pentecost are reminders of the rhythmic pauses that God built into the flow of time. Though the ancients divided the lunar month into four quarters of seven days each, it is the divine mandate of Exodus 20 and Deuteronomy 5 that has given the week its prominence in Western civilization.

Three commands sum up the text. First, *keep the Sabbath holy* (vv. 12–14a). The obvious response is, How? No mention of corporate worship, of offering or sacrifice is included. The holiness of the day is defined simply and directly: "In it you shall not do any work" (v. 14).

This definition is a reminder of what *holy* means: set apart from everyday life and reserved for the special purposes of God. As priests were called apart from workers and farmers to supervise Israel's worship, so too the seventh day was to be separated from the other six by the absence of work or, more positively, by the presence of rest.

The seriousness of God's requirement shows up in the text's second command: *Include the whole household* (v. 14b). The order to rest was not for the privileged elite, who could relax and enjoy a day off at the expense of children, slaves, or aliens. All work was to cease—even donkeys were to shed their burdens and oxen and cattle to be loosed from their yokes.

God, the Lord of time, built into the calendar the reminder of our dependence on him. Though labor we must in cooperation with his providence, life ultimately depends more on his providence than on our labor.

The fullest reason for our rest is the third command: *Remember the grand rescue* (v. 15). Exodus says, you rest because God rested when he finished the creation (Exod. 20:11); Deuteronomy says, you rest because, when you were slaves in Egypt, not allowed to rest, God rescued you. And because our redemption by the cross and resurrection forms the New Testament parallel to the redemption from Egypt, this whole understanding of the Sabbath rest has been transferred to the Christian understanding of Sunday, the first day of the week, and the day of resurrection.

The Sabbath was not so much geared to human need as to divine activity, commemorating God's sovereignty in creation and his invincible power ("mighty hand"; "outstretched arm"; v. 15) in redemption. Rescued slaves must never undervalue the privilege of rest; it is a gift of God's redemptive grace. Emancipated serfs we are, as God's people. Never can we deprive others of the right, even of the obligation, to rest. Our society, both workaholic and leisure-crazed, is in jeopardy of dismissing God's providence and spurning God's grace in its frenzied efforts to achieve and escape. It needs to hear with joyful seriousness the command to rest.

One thing more. The church of God historically has seen the Sabbath or Sunday rest as a preview of the eternal rest that awaits the people of God. When the creation has fulfilled its purpose, when the rescue of the human family from its bondage has reached its consummation, there remains a rest, an ultimate Sabbath, for those who love God (Heb. 4:9–10; Rev. 14:13).

SECOND LESSON: 2 CORINTHIANS 4:5–12

Paul's integrity was under fire. The congregation at Corinth seemed to have no lack of ambitious leaders ready to elevate their own prestige by assaulting Paul's message, motives, methods, and call. The first five chapters of the letter have as their chief purpose the defense of Paul's integrity and authority.

Of his detractors Paul could say with Joseph, "As for you, you meant evil against me; but God meant it for good" (Gen. 50:20). And to that, we who have profited so abundantly from Paul's defense can join our "Amen."

Paul's first test of the integrity of ministry was the content of the message: *Christ's lordship in contrast to our servitude* (v. 5). The two halves of the contrast are crucial. No ministry that does not exalt Jesus as living Lord of the church, the world, indeed of the universe, can merit the label Christian. It was not superior knowledge that Paul lauded, nor spiritual experiences, nor miraculous powers. It was Jesus Christ, God's Messiah, the fulfillment of all God's mission through Israel, to whom was ascribed the title of Lord, echoing the majesty of the divine name Yahweh and contradicting the Caesars' blasphemous claims to deity.

We can embrace Jesus' lordship only from our knees. To name him Lord of all is to brand ourselves his slaves. Strikingly, Paul attached "your" not "his" to the word "servant": (1) to remind the Corinthians of how faithfully he had tried to meet their needs; (2) to teach us that one way in which persons come to acknowledge Jesus as Lord is through our service to them. This all goes on "for Jesus' sake" (v. 5). As God's Servant he set the pace for our servitude (Mark 10:42–45); whatever we do for the least of his brethren we do to him (Matt. 25:40).

Paul's second test of integrity was the motivation of the mission: *God's glory in contrast to our commonness* (vv. 6–9). Paul's conversion to Jesus the Lord was not the result of a ponderous quest for religious truth. It shattered his darkness with a brilliance comparable only to the first day of creation, when God called light into being and snatched the gloomy shroud from the face of the deep (Gen. 1:2–3). And what Paul saw was nothing less than God's own glory revealed in the face of the risen Christ (v. 6; Acts 9:3–6; 1 Cor. 15:8). This divine surprise so confronted him with God's grace that his life's purpose was transformed from the darkness of persecuting the church to the light of proclaiming the gospel to the Gentiles.

Yet he saw himself as the same common person with no more intrinsic value to the mission than the pottery jug that stores a treasure. (v. 7). If Jews discovered that Jesus was their Messiah, if Gentiles turned to God from idols, it was God's work not his.

Paul reveled in his frailty (2 Cor. 12:9b). So fearful was he of taking credit for God's work, so disdainful of every arrogance of religious leaders who detracted from the grace of the gospel, that he celebrated Christian commonness as purposeful, "to show that the transcendent power belongs to God and not to us" (v. 7).

The delicate balance between the divine glory that moved Paul to mission and the common clay through which that glory worked is illustrated in vv. 8–9. Paul minces no words in describing the effects of opposition to his preaching: afflicted, perplexed, persecuted, struck down—all present participles in Greek to show that these were continual happenings not random episodes. Our human frailty is highly vulnerable in a fallen world that resents the gospel more readily than it accepts it.

Yet the transcendent power of God has assured the survival of God's mission. We are not crushed, not driven to despair, not forsaken, not destroyed. Clay we may be. But the powerful treasure bestowed upon us gives the clay a steely resilience.

Paul's third test of integrity was the context of our activity: *Jesus' vitality in contrast with our suffering* (vv. 10–12). The church's task goes on under the shadow of death. Four times in three verses we hear the words death or mortal, and just as frequently, the words life and live.

The lesson's climax is the interplay between these words. When Christ the Lord is the content of our message and the glory of God in Jesus is our motivation, then we are called to identify with the suffering that marked all of Jesus' earthly life and culminated on the cross. The world that dealt with him by apathy, insult, and rejection has not yet been transformed. His body, the church, yet suffers with him, not to atone for sin but to complete the mission.

Paul's identification with the Lord's human suffering is placarded in the fourfold use of the name Jesus (vv. 10–12). That suffering had life-releasing power like a vial that had to be broken before the medicine could be applied. Paul was realistic, not sarcastic, when he summed up the mystery of God's use of persecution to spark salvation: "So death is at work in us (as we share Jesus' sufferings), but life in you (as you believe in him as Lord and Savior, just as we already have believed)" (v. 12).

GOSPEL: MARK 2:23-28

Controversy frames the context for this story. It is the fourth in a series of five encounters with scribes or Pharisees that Mark recounts: (1) what right does Jesus have to forgive sin? (2:1–12); (2) why does he eat with tax collectors and sinners? (2:13–17); (3) why do not Jesus' disciples fast like John's? (2:18–22); (4) why do Jesus and his disciples pluck grain on the Sabbath? (2:23–28); (5) how can Jesus perform healings on the Sabbath? (3:1–6).

Mark uses the controversies to teach about the gospel's radical character, which is his major theme (1:1). They highlight Jesus' authority to break with past interpretations of the faith and to demonstrate the presence of the kingdom of God (1:15). There was nothing trivial nor petty about these controversies: forgiving sins was a blasphemous usurping of God's right (2:7); table fellowship with sinners threatened the purity of the faith (2:16); fasting was an important demonstration of spiritual discipline (2:18); Sabbath keeping was both a divine command and a key expression of Jewish uniqueness (2:24; 3:2; Exod. 31:15, where death is the prescribed punishment for its violation).

Jesus' rejoinders do not brand these issues as trite. His tack is that the urgency of the kingdom gives him the right to do things differently from the set patterns. The Messianic mission is not merely new content placed in old containers: "New wine is for fresh skins" (v. 22).

The *accusation* is based on two violations of Sabbath law, which had been greatly embellished by rabbinic teachings. (See the lengthy tractates in the Mishnah and Talmud.) The first violation finds Jesus and his men not out on a casual stroll but actually journeying, probably on their way to another place of ministry in Galilee, perhaps traveling light, carrying little provision for the road (cf. 6:7–8). Their itinerary may have taken them well beyond the limits for a "Sabbath day's journey," stipulated in Jewish law—two thousand cubits or approximately three-fifths of a mile (cf. Acts 1:12).

The second violation was plucking the grain (v. 23), an act interpreted as tantamount to harvesting, whereas the embellishments of the law forbade the picking or preparing of food on the Sabbath (Exod. 16:5). The Pharisees felt the religious stability of their whole society shaken by the most influential teacher since the days of the prophets.

Jesus' *defense* against the accusation began with a historical precedent: the story of David's emergency actions in devouring the sacred bread that was displayed before the Lord and then eaten by the priests alone (1 Sam. 21:1–6). The parallels between the two stories make clear Jesus' point. He was not saying that anyone has the right to break the law in a crisis. He was deliberately connecting his circumstances with David's: David, like Jesus, (1) was the rightful but unrecognized king, (2) was on a mission authorized by God to give the kingdom an entirely new expression, (3) had to have sustenance to carry out this commission, and (4) shared the meal with his companions. Mark's story makes its point: The Son of David, God's Messiah, is present to announce and inaugurate the kingdom, history's most urgent assignment.

The historical precedent is reinforced by a fundamental principle: Jesus, even though he may look like a mere mortal (the probable meaning here of Son of man, v. 28), is Lord of everything, including the Sabbath, and has the right to decide how the Sabbath is best to be used.

No ticket for license in the use of the Lord's day is issued here. True, the Sabbath was instituted, partly at least, for human welfare, but it is even more true that our use of it is defined by kingdom purposes as dictated by the Lord of the kingdom.

The resurrection of Jesus and the outpouring of the Spirit at Pentecost impelled the early believers to celebrate their worship on Sunday, along with, or rather than Saturday. Thus, they encouraged most Christians through the centuries to follow their lead and so to symbolize the change from the Old Covenant to the New in the calendar of worship. The calendar change substantiates not nullifies the importance of the Sabbath: God's people yet need to celebrate the new creation as well as the old, to commemorate the redemption of the cross as well as that of the exodus, to encourage rest for themselves and their household, and above all to rejoice in the kingdom of the Son of man who came to give us rest (Matt. 11:28–29).

The Third Sunday After Pentecost

Lutheran	Roman Catholic	Episcopal	Pres/UCC/Chr	Meth/COCU
Gen. 3:9–15	Gen. 3:9–15	Gen. 3:(1–7), 8–21	Gen. 3:9–15	Gen. 3:1–21
2 Cor. 4:13–18	2 Cor. 4:13—5:1	2 Cor. 4:13–18	2 Cor. 4:13—5:1	2 Cor. 4:13—5:1
Mark 3:20–35	Mark 3:20–35	Mark 3:20–35	Mark 3:20–35	Mark 3:20–35

FIRST LESSON: GENESIS 3:9–15

The beginning of this scene symbolizes a turning point in human experience. The primeval man and woman have bought the serpent's lie and defied the Lord God's authority. The lure of forbidden fruit and the lust of godlike wisdom were temptations too heady to resist. The woman and the man ate and with that meal first tasted the bitterness of shame and fear (Gen. 3:1–8). Their delightful nakedness (2:25) now made them uneasy; the garden that was their domain now became their hide-out.

Into that setting, with his plan so dreadfully violated, walks the Lord God with a cluster of *insistent divine questions* (vv. 9, 11, 13). The switch in grammar mirrors the change in relationships. The fiats of creation, the evaluations that all is good, the commands to control the earth, the promise of a helper—these yield to the interrogative mood. Things have gone wrong and the Lord God has a right to know why. And he presses the confrontation with a tenacity that demonstrates his authority.

With the questions comes an intimation of grace. At a time when embarrassment and anxiety have sent the human couple into hiding, the Lord God takes the initiative to find them. And that note of grace may be present in the first question which has little bite to it: "Where are you?" (v. 9). It gave the pair opportunity to reveal themselves with minimal pain.

The divine questions are met with a series of *evasive human answers*. The couple failed to use the space the Lord God offered them to give the real reason for their seclusion. Like his offspring since, the first man dealt with the symptom not the cause: "I was afraid, because I was naked; and I hid myself" (v. 10). Fear and shame are more readily confessed than sin.

The divine Questioner now takes away all space and crowds the man with back-to-back questions (v. 11), one indirect—"Who told you that you were naked?"—and one direct—"Have you eaten of the tree?" The only possible cause of the man's shame is his sin. The first question led inevitably to the second. Its specific reminder of the divine command (2:17) puts the man directly on the spot. He hedges his confession—"And I ate"—by blaming the woman explicitly for giving him the fruit and by blaming God implicitly for giving him the woman (v. 12).

Next, the Lord God pursues the matter with the woman, who admits the deed and blames the serpent (v. 13). The whole scene holds sad promise for the human future. The couple, created and commissioned to "have dominion . . . over every living thing that moves upon the earth" (Gen. 1:28), slough off their responsibility and force the Lord

God who had blessed them to become their prosecutor and their judge.

The pervasive divine judgment addressed itself first to the serpent (vv. 14–15), who is banned from normal animal life and consigned to a career of dusty crawling. But more important, the serpent's judgment spills over to afflict the human family. Enmity is to be the relationship between serpents and people right on through the generations. Each party will be bruised by the other—the serpent in the head; the woman's children in the heel.

That perpetual enmity marks the serpent as a symbol of evil, held accountable for a role in the temptation and destined for a continued role in the human struggle to come to grips with God's creative purposes. The Revelation identifies the serpent with Satan (Rev. 12:9) and reads more into Genesis than is there. But, given the millennia of battle with the influences of evil—personal, social, and institution-al—that have marked human history, we can understand why.

This is a story of volcanic disruptions. Life's basic relationships are blown apart: human beings hide from the God who made them; a man protects his reputation at the expense of the woman he so deeply desires; a woman degrades herself to the level of an animal by declaring herself weaker than the serpent; the Creator condemns his own handiwork to harsh and prolonged judgment. Where else can we find in so few words the explanation for so much of what is wrong with our existence?

And where else can we find a beginning of an answer to those wrongs? God has asked his damning questions; God has pronounced his awesome sentences; the creatures stand guilty. Yet God is still there.

SECOND LESSON: 2 CORINTHIANS 4:13–18

Paul's defense of his apostleship (2 Corinthians 1—5) gives him opportunity to interpret the implications of Christian life and ministry to the Corinthian congregation. Here, as in 4:5–12, his thought centers in the contrast between present affliction and future glory. Paul's aim is straightforward: he wants to make sure that suffering and persecution cause the church neither to doubt his apostleship nor to fear its future.

The tension between the now and the not yet is a familiar experience of God's people. Hebrew slaves groaned in oppression hoping for their own land. Israelite worshipers marched through towns throttled by injustice to pray in the Temple for God to crown their king with justice. Weary Jews slogged to Palestine from exile only to wonder when God would fulfill his promises of a bright tomorrow. Black Americans sang both "Nobody Knows the Trouble I've Seen" and "Goin' to Walk All Over God's Heaven."

To that tension our lesson speaks. Its argument is like stages in a relay race: each thought passes its point like a baton to the next runner; the final pass carries the argument to the finish line which is also the starting place.

The race is about faith and how to maintain it in the face of persecution. In stage one, Paul speaks of *a faith that leads to witness* (v. 13). The apostle finds a kindred soul in the psalmist who spoke of faith in the midst of affliction and lived to sing a song of thanksgiving (Ps. 116:10). The faith that sustained Paul could not be silenced no matter how tight the screws of persecution turned. The reality of God's presence with him prompted him to witness to the works of God and the hope they sparked, whatever his circumstances. With his psalmist, Paul would pay God his vows before his people (Ps. 116:18).

He had unshakable ground for confidence, as he argues in stage two, defining his message as *a witness that testifies to resurrection* (v. 14). The resurrection of Jesus is the guarantee that nothing and no one will ultimately thwart God's purposes. Jesus' resurrection gave Paul's faith a solid historical foundation. But more, he viewed it not as an isolated episode in holy history but as the overture to a divine opera whose plot is the resurrection of all of Adam's sons and daughters (1 Cor. 15:20–23). One of the grand results of that performance is that all of God's people will be united before him—"and bring us with you into his presence" (v. 14). Whatever barrier may separate us now—geography, persecution, theological interpretation, even death—will tumble before the power of resurrection, just as graveclothes were once stripped off and a sealed stone was rolled aside.

In stage three, Paul depicts *a resurrection that results in glory* (v. 15). The apostolic mission, with its faith in the face of trial and its proclamation of resurrection in the teeth of death, is not for the sake of the apostles but for the church. The church's life is changed, its destiny assured by what God has done and will do through Christ. This is the gospel's nearer purpose. Its further mission is God's glory, which is enhanced as multitudes taste his grace and join the chorus of all who respond with the only reply fitting to our helplessness and his beneficence, "Thank you." Again Paul may have remembered the psalmist's example: "I will offer to thee the sacrifice of thanksgiving" (Ps. 116:17).

In stage four, the race returns to its start, when Paul depicts *a glory that nurtures faith* (vv. 16–18). The hope of resurrection buoys our confidence in what God will do. And part of what he will do is to prepare for us "an eternal weight of glory beyond all comparison" (v. 17). We who seek to praise God's glory will live to share that glory, in all its priceless worth ("weight of glory" echoes the Hebrew *kābôd*, which marks glory as something weighty and therefore worthwhile). This talk of glory has magnificent practical consequences: it keeps us from losing heart (v. 16), and it fixes our eyes on faith's only suitable target, the unseen things that are eternal (v. 18; cf. Heb. 11:1).

The race has gone full circle: faith has led to witness, which has testified to resurrection, which has resulted in glory, which has nurtured faith. But the race is no idle exercise. Reasons for faith, incentives to faith, results of faith have been clarified. And our faith, if we too have run these four stages, is the stronger.

GOSPEL: MARK 3:20–35

This story is about responses and relationships to Jesus. Actually, there are two stories, one wrapped around the other: a story of Jesus' relationship to his family (vv. 20–21, 31–35) and a story about Jesus' response to his opponents (vv. 22–30). Like the parable of the seed and soils that follows it (4:1–9), the lesson demonstrates the various types of receptions experienced by the presence of God's kingdom in Jesus. And, in turn, it describes Jesus' response to each reception. Three parties are involved: Jesus' relatives, scribal opponents, disciples.

Jesus' *relatives* received the news of the kingdom with *embarrassment*. Red-faced at reports of his claims, his wonders, and his controversies, they tried to hustle him into hiding. No family enjoys hearing that a loved one "is beside himself" (v. 21). Few stories illustrate better the reality of the incarnation, the fully human life of the Son of God, than this. His own mother and brothers boggled at his mission (v. 31).

Jesus' response was to *ignore them* (vv. 32–33). He practiced kingdom priorities as truly as he preached them (Matt. 10:34–38). Love for family, even honor of mother (Exod. 20:12; Deut. 5:16), had to take second place.

Jesus' *opponents* greet the works of the kingdom with *blasphemy*. No mere derangement nor psychotic behavior can account for his power over demons. The scribes read him as nothing less than Satan's agent (v. 22). Beelzebub is a particularly insulting figure to be associated with, whether the name is connected with the Canaanite "lord of the high place" or the more earthy translation "lord of the dung." This mammoth misunderstanding leaves Jesus no choice but to summon his opponents and seek to set them straight.

His response is to *rebuke them* (vv. 23–30). To do this he uses an assortment of verbal weaponry: (1) a rhetorical question whose answer is so obvious that his hearers must have felt stupid—"How can Satan cast out Satan?" (v. 23); (2) a two-pronged parable about kingdoms and houses divided against themselves (vv. 24–25); (3) an application of the parable to Satan, so that his hearers can make no mistake about its meaning (v. 26); (4) a parable intended to explain Jesus' purpose in casting out demons—namely to limit Satan's power so that the kingdom can be planted (v. 27); (5) a warning about the danger of blaspheming against the Spirit by crediting the Spirit's work done in Jesus (1:10) to the power of the enemy.

Jesus' *disciples* (see 2:13–19), whose role the story deliberately underplays, turn out to be the heroes, participating in the kingdom tasks with *obedience*. They busy themselves with Jesus, not even finding time to eat (3:20). They sit with him while he teaches, open to his instruction about the new kingdom and the will of God which is its constitution (vv. 32, 34–35).

The response of Jesus was *to adopt them*. They were to become his true family. He who came to do God's will declared himself kin to all who share that purpose.

This story is linked to the First Lesson (Gen. 3:9–15): a new family dedicated to God's will is undoing the work of our disobedient parents; new power is unleashed through Jesus to defeat the evil that posed the first temptation; new relationships of caring and commitment are formed among Christ's loved ones. The loss of paradise is not irreparable. In Jesus and his family, there has come to be something even better.

The Fourth Sunday After Pentecost

Lutheran	Roman Catholic	Episcopal	Pres/UCC/Chr	Meth/COCU
Ezek. 17:22–24	Ezek. 17:22–24	Ezek. 31:1–6, 10–14	Ezek. 17:22–24	Ezek. 17:22–24
2 Cor. 5:1–10	2 Cor. 5:6–10	2 Cor. 5:1–10	2 Cor. 5:6–10	2 Cor. 5:1–10
Mark 4:26–34	Mark 4:26–34	Mark 4:26–34	Mark 4:26–34	Mark 4:26–34

FIRST LESSON: EZEKIEL 17:22–24

This is a picture of divine sovereignty. The promise is conveyed in imagery: a sprig is snipped from a cedar; a twig is snapped from the sprig and planted; a mighty tree grows from the twig; the surrounding trees watch and learn a lesson. The Lord God controls the whole process: he does the snipping and planting (v. 22), nurtures the new tree's prosperity (v. 23), teaches the other trees the lesson of his lordship, and seals the promise with his own confirmation (v. 24).

God's sovereign initiative is stressed: "I myself will take a sprig" (v. 22). The "I myself" contrasts with what Ezekiel has just pictured (17:1–21). Plucking and planting are there ascribed to two great eagles. The first eagle (vv. 3–6) is Babylon (note vv. 12–14), which snatched Judah's king Jehoiachin in 597 B.C., settled him in Babylon, and planted Zedekiah as monarch in his place (2 Kings 24:10–17). The second eagle (vv. 7–8) is Egypt (vv. 15–17), which sought to woo Zedekiah away from allegiance to Babylon and hastened Judah's destruction—a destruction which the Lord freely owns as his judgment on the treacherous Zedekiah (vv. 19–21).

Now God himself sovereignly does the plucking and planting, not the two imperial powers. And he acts under the guise of an eagle—the imagery that controls the riddle or fable (animals and plants are the chief actors) of 17:1–10. The messenger formula (v. 22) names the Name of the sovereign planter and thus unveils the most important fact in the promise: the Lord will carry it out, despite or through or above all political machinations.

God's sovereign achievement is conveyed by the growth of the tree (v. 23). Again we catch the contrast: Egypt uprooted Babylon's plant (vv. 7–8), and Babylon, in turn, struck Egypt's plant and withered it like an east wind (v. 10). Not so with God's planting: he chooses the right place, the "mountain height of Israel," probably Mount Zion in Jerusalem (cf. 20:40); he fosters the growth of a noble cedar, like the best of Lebanon, with ample shade for animals and nesting space for birds.

Because God, not human rulers, has done the planting and site selecting, the permanence of the growth is assured. Not so with Tyre's prince, who lived "on the holy mountain of God" but was cast out (28:14) for corruption, or with Egypt's king who was mighty as a Lebanon cedar but was hewn down for pride (31:2–12).

God's sovereign surprise is the high note (v. 24). As usual in Ezekiel, God has a major lesson to teach about his lordship in history. This time his point centers in his power to bring surprising change: "I the Lord bring low the high tree, and make high the low tree, dry up the green tree, and make the dry tree flourish." Like Hannah before him (1 Sam. 2:1–10), like Mary after him (Luke 1:46–55), Ezekiel exulted in the Lord's way of crushing independence and arrogance and honoring trust and humility.

The text is not about horticulture but messianic politics. The twig that God tends is a king (as in 17:4, 12); the flourishing cedar is his restored kingdom; the trees that come to know how surprisingly the Lord works are neighbor kingdoms. Like Isaiah ("a shoot from the stump of Jesse"; 11:1) and Jeremiah ("I will raise up for David a righteous branch"; 23:5), Ezekiel uses the language of husbandry to describe both the new thing God will do in establishing his kingdom and its continuity with the throne of David (2 Samuel 7). God signed his promise with a bold assertion: "And I will do it" (v. 24). We who worship him through David's greater Son know just how well he has done it.

SECOND LESSON: 2 CORINTHIANS 5:1–10.

The topic is death and how to deal with it. The menace of persecution hangs over the text. The badgering and battering of adversaries (4:8–9), the sharing of Jesus' sufferings (4:10–12) keep Paul in mind of mortality. So do the anxieties of the Corinthians who worry about their own destiny and that of their apostle. The passage is complicated, but its overall message is straightforward: God has a plan for our tomorrow that keeps us steady to serve him today.

The first half of the lesson rings with Paul's *firm confidence of the future* (vv. 1–5)—"We know," he begins. No stargazing, no visionary guessing here. Solid knowledge is what Paul claims, knowledge born of his understanding of God's character and the Spirit's presence (v. 5).

That confidence is bolstered by *the hope of an eternal home* (vv. 1–4). Groans (v. 2) and sighs (v. 4) are the catchwords of our tentlike humanity, especially where that humanity is pressured by misunderstanding and rejection of the faith. The eternal home is described very differently: building, house (v. 1), additional outer garment (v. 4). Best of all it is not handmade (v. 1), and it is radiant with life (v. 4).

The most direct interpretation runs somewhat like this: when believers die, life goes on, freed from anxiety and anguish, in God's presence; death, then, does not leave us naked or unclothed (vv. 3–4), that is, stripped of dignity and hope and meaning, but only ushers us into the divine dwelling (like the "Father's house" with its "many rooms," John 14:2), which is unassailable by all that erodes our earthly bodies; we become those whom Paul calls "the dead in Christ" who await the resurrection and who are promised the privilege to "rise first" (1 Thess. 4:16). Paul's two sets of metaphors, therefore, mean essentially the same thing: (1) the destroyed tent, the body, is superseded by a building or house; (2) this protection is further described as additional clothing wrapped around our mortality, so absorbing it that life not death becomes our crowning characteristic (v. 4).

Paul's confidence is grounded in *the hope of divine preparation* (v. 5). As mystifying as this change of situation and mode of living may be, we need not doubt its reality, because God has sent the Spirit to dwell within us. The Spirit is the presence of the future in God's people, the Representative of tomorrow's perfection in the midst of today's infirmities. "Guarantee" is like a large down payment on a significant purchase or an engagement ring as the symbol of a permanent commitment.

The second half of the lesson resounds with Paul's *good courage in the present* (vv. 6–10). The groans and sighs are there. And so is the sense of incompleteness in fellowship with God, despite all that we enjoy of his comfort and strength through the Spirit: as long as the fragile body is still our home, we do not experience the fullness of Christ's presence ("We are away from the Lord," v. 6). Yet this separation does not defeat us.

We can take courage *to walk by faith* (v. 7), even when we do not yet see all that future glory. Faith is not ignorance or foolishness or futility. Given by the Spirit and grounded in Jesus' death and resurrection, it carries its own assurance. It is no less certain than sight; it just does not catch the picture so brightly. Faith is like the sure knowledge, treasured by a college student on the homebound train, that mom and dad will greet her with smiles and hugs; sight is like getting there and having it happen.

We can take courage *to wait for God's timing* (vv. 8–9). Paul stands ready at any time to swap the ills of the body for the joys of the Lord's presence. Yet the when of this swap-meet is not in his hands. He has made his preference clear. The rest is up to God.

We can take courage *to aim to please God* (v. 9). Waiting and loafing are not the same thing. Life's purpose on earth or in heaven is to serve God's glory, celebrate his love, magnify his name. We do that *now* in the face of frailty and hostility; we shall continue to do that *then* in a setting of radiance and fellowship.

We can take courage *to prepare for judgment* (v. 10). Heaven involves accountability as well as fellowship. True, we are justified by faith and Christ is our righteousness. But Christian freedom is not a license that allows us to live like pagans; it is a passport to a new realm of responsibility to worship, love, serve, witness, and wait (1 Thess. 1:10). Whether we are Christ's people or not is decided by faith in him as a gift of God's grace; how we live out the discipleship daily while we wait for the hope of glory is what Christ will look at when we stand before him.

This remarkable example of Paul's firm confidence of the future and good courage in the present is the best remedy we have for dealing with death. With him all Christ's people can say, "For to me to live is Christ, and to die is gain" (Phil. 1:21).

GOSPEL: MARK 4:26–34

The discrepancy was huge. Jesus' opponents must have scoffed at it; Jesus' followers must have worried about it. They heard all the talk about God's kingdom yet they saw only an artisan from Nazareth with a small crew of motley men, the chief of whom were Galilean fishers. The discrepancy was huge. No wealth, no weaponry, no pedigree marked that team as royalty. To address this discrepancy Jesus spoke these two parables. His points are clear: the kingdom's growth is the work of God (vv. 26–29); from tiny beginnings God brings grand results (vv. 30–32).

The first parable, found only in Mark, describes how seed grows secretly and silently while the farmer sleeps or goes about his daily routines. Through the story, Jesus proclaims one main idea: *The kingdom of God is achieved by God's power.* Detail after detail conspires to underscore this. The farmer (here just called "a man," v. 26) plays a part only at the beginning in scattering the seed and at the end in harvesting (v. 29); in between he is described as caught in the cycle of rising and sleeping, as though he pays no attention whatsoever to the seed, ignorant even of how it grows. Meanwhile, both the seed (v. 27) and the land (v. 28) go about their divinely ordered tasks without human aid or supervision: the seed sprouts and grows; the soil by itself (the Greek is *automatē)* nudges and nurtures the growth through its successive states from blade to ear to full grain.

The mention of the man tells us that we as human beings have a role to play in the kingdom's extension, while it warns us against overestimating that role. The reference to the harvest promises us that God's plan will succeed, while it urges us to do our part. But the bulk of the work and the force of the story rest with the seed and the soil whose wondrous ways of growing things are in God's charge. The answer to the discrepancy between talk of the kingdom and the looks of the kingdom lies in the strong and silent hands of God.

The second parable (found also in Matt. 13:31–32 and Luke 13:18–19) describes the amazing way in which a mustard seed blossoms into a huge shrub. Jesus teaches that *the kingdom of God will grow to grand proportions.* Since Jesus' aim was not to teach botany, we interpret his descriptions of "the smallest of all the seeds on earth" (v. 31) and "the greatest of all shrubs" (v. 32) in terms of their literary effect. By any standard, however, the mustard seed's growth is amazing: shrubs in Galilee can measure eight or ten feet high.

Both of these parables draw on the message of the First Lesson (Ezek. 17:22–24). The cedar tree there started very small, only a snippet from a sprig, and grew to rule the forest. And it did that with divine nurture not human ingenuity. Moreover, like the cedar tree, the mustard shrub shelters and shades the birds of the air. Jesus may be suggesting that Ezekiel's promise of Israel's growth despite Babylonian and Egyptian opposition has now come true in Jesus' announcement of the new kingdom.

An intriguing connection this is between Ezekiel's imagery and Jesus'. The prophet used the twig to symbolize a son of David destined to rule in might and majesty in place of the captured Jehoiachin and the rebellious Zedekiah. Then, half a millennium later, another Son of David adapted the story to apply to the kingdom which he inaugurated. Implicitly, Jesus was saying what Ezekiel foresaw is now here, and there is yet more to come.

The discrepancy was huge. At times it still seems that way when we compare the powerful organizations of industry, education, or government to the struggling groups of Christians with whom we worship. We can look at our churches and wonder how well the name "kingdom of God" suits them. That is why the two parables are there. They still may baffle the multitudes. But they are always at hand for Christ's disciples who discern their word and take heart: God is about his work; his kingdom will thrive.

The Fifth Sunday After Pentecost

Lutheran	Roman Catholic	Episcopal	Pres/UCC/Chr	Meth/COCU
Job 38:1–11	Job 38:1, 8–11	Job 38:1–11, 16–18	Job 38:1–11	Job 38:1–11, 16–18
2 Cor. 5:14–21	2 Cor. 5:14–17	2 Cor. 5:14–21	2 Cor. 5:16–21	2 Cor. 5:14–21
Mark 4:35–41	Mark 4:35–41	Mark 4:35–41; (5:1–20)	Mark 4:35–41	Mark 4:35—5:20

FIRST LESSON: JOB 38:1–11

The question mark is the dominant punctuation of Job—not in numbers, perhaps, but certainly in influence. The Lord himself sets the tone with his questions of the Satan: "Whence have you come?"

(1:7) and "Have you considered my servant Job?" (1:8). Satan's reply is interrogative in mood: "Does Job fear God for naught?" (1:9). When the rack of suffering is stretched as Satan puts Job's faith to the test, Job's wife joins the questioning chorus: "Do you still hold fast your integrity?" (2:9). And Job answers with a counterquestion: "Shall we receive good at the hand of God, and shall we not receive evil?" (2:10).

But when the first pangs of suffering settle into long aches, Job's tone changes, though question is still his mode of communication: "Why did I not die at birth, come forth from the womb and expire?" (3:11). The friends reply in kind: "Think now, who that was innocent ever perished?" (4:7, Eliphaz). Then Job's rebuttals may be couched in question marks: "Shall windy words have an end? Or what provokes you that you answer?" (16:3). But when the argument seems to reach an impasse the poet poses a key query, aimed equally at Job and the friends: "But where shall wisdom be found? And where is the place of understanding?" (28:12). Elihu follows suit: "Who has prescribed for him (God) his way, or who can say, 'Thou hast done wrong'?" (36:23).

The interrogative mood fits the style and message of Job. Much of the style is dialogue—God and the Satan at the beginning, God and Job at the end, and the friends and Job in between. By artfully forming the question, the speaker can either determine the opponent's answer or silence him. The question-form also highlights the mysteries of the book—mysteries best expressed as questions: Does God have freedom to ask Job to suffer and not tell him why? Does Job have faith to bear both his suffering and God's silence?

The unraveling of the mystery, when the Lord answers Job, comes not by announcement or explanation but by further questions, a tightly packed bundle of them that determines the tone of the two great divine speeches (38:1–40; 40:6—41:34). A look at these questions—their use, their tone, their content—gives us glimpses as to what God intends Job and us to understand about the wonders of his ways with us.

The *fact of the questions* shows how personally God cares for Job. He owed him no answer; he is God not a human being; he has full right to guard his mysteries. But he came to answer (v. 1) and treated Job with dignity when he challenged him to answer in turn (v. 3). Person to person runs the conversation—the *I* to the *you* (v. 3; 40:3–4). So great is God's grace, so freely does he stoop to human need, that he talks with Job as directly as had Eliphaz, Zophar, and Bildad.

The *tone of the questions* shows how much Job has yet to learn: "Who is this that darkens counsel by words without knowledge?" (v. 2); "Where were you when I laid the foundation of the earth?" God speaks with the authority of the teacher and asks from Job the docility of the pupil. He establishes the right to instruct Job in matters beyond Job's ken and needles him a bit—"Tell me, if you have understanding, . . . surely you know!" (vv. 4–5)—to sharpen his readiness to learn.

The *content of the questions* is surprising: (1) no reference is made to any previous discussion in the book; God finds all the friend's weighty arguments and all Job's brilliant complaints irrelevant; (2) no finger of blame is pointed at Satan who first proposed the test; God shouldered the whole responsibility for Job's affliction; (3) no accusation of sin is voiced; God tacitly affirmed Job's protest of innocence (chap. 31); (4) no direct explanation of the suffering was offered; Job was still being asked to walk by faith; (5) no account is ventured of God's sovereignty in human affairs; the lessons of creation, the wonders of God's world, were to carry over and become bridges to trust when history and human experience became laden with problems.

The Lord who laid the earth's foundations with such delightful precision that the angels ("sons of God"; 1:6) and stars joined in chorus to celebrate the construction (38:4–7), the Lord who gave birth to the sea and swaddled it in clouds (vv. 8–11), is powerful, wise, and trustworthy. Job had not been present then as Wisdom was (Prov. 8:22–31). But with the help of God's questions he learned the lessons of humility before the Creator's majesty and trust in the Creator's power (42:1–6).

SECOND LESSON: 2 CORINTHIANS 5:14–21

The differences between Paul and his detractors were not trivial. They could not be patched up like slight disagreements or eased by knowing each other better. Instead, he helped the Corinthians grasp how huge the differences were. To do this he painted massive theological backdrops, covered with scenes of the divine plan for the redemption of the human family and the restoration of all that had been cursed because of sinful rebellion. Against those canvases the opposition of the false apostles took on its proper perspectives: their vaunted wisdom was unmasked as foolishness; their superior knowledge was exposed as ignorance; their claims to serve were shown up as selfishness.

The root problem that Paul was trying to correct was *the old discrimination*. The clue to this is found in v. 12, where the troublemakers are described: "Those who pride themselves on a man's position and not on his heart." Such a judgment would come as a surprise to the Greek world where family, station, wealth, and office were so highly valued. Common workers (like tentmakers!), slaves, and foreigners were scarcely given the time of day by the landed gentry, the wealthy merchants, or the intellectual leaders.

The adversaries of the gospel were apparently taking this tack with Paul, demeaning his importance by making light of his vocation, his appearance, his behavior. The apostle knew their problem firsthand. He had once lived that way himself, limited in perspectives to a "human point of view" even in his evaluation of Jesus (v. 16). Apparently, before his conversion he had summarily dismissed all attempts to hail Jesus as Messiah as misguided wishes of unthinking people. The simplicity of Jesus' life, the humbleness of his origins, and the ignominy of his death all argued powerfully against any messianic claims.

But now Paul knew better. He had been released from the limits of the old discrimination, practiced by his namesake: "For the Lord sees not as man sees; man looks on the outward appearance, but the Lord looks on the heart" (1 Sam. 16:7). He had entered into the freedom of *the new creation*. The old ways of courting the powerful and spurning the useless have passed away. A whole new view of life has come into being in which Christ's people see not only Jesus but every one, including themselves, in an entirely different light.

For one thing, *we are controlled by the love that Christ has shown* in dying for us (v. 14). Our outlook and motives have been reshaped by the awareness that his death is our death. He died in our place and was raised. What sensible alternative do we have but to live not for ourselves—fawning over those who seem powerful or attractive, coveting their goods and reputation, elevating our own prestige by stepping on the heads of the less fortunate—but for the one who died in our stead (v. 15)? Life, then, is no longer out of control as was the old discrimination but is fitted into the total plan that God has for the renewal of the universe. In Christ we participate in the new creation that will outdo even the wonders of the old creation that God displayed to Job (chaps. 38—41). And the rule of the new creation is not raw power but holy love, the love of Christ for us, of us for Christ and one another.

For another thing the new creation prompts us to see that *we are commissioned to call for reconciliation.* Our share in the new creation, our release from the old discrimination, is the gift of God through the reconciliation accomplished by Jesus' death and resurrection (v. 18). Without a comma to slow him down, Paul describes the inevitable consequence of God's work, "and gave us the ministry of reconciliation" (v. 18).

Not that we do the reconciliation; even the new creation does not equip us for that. But we are appointed as ambassadors with the authority and the knowledge to speak for God and to urge others to come to terms with him through Christ (vv. 19–20) who bore the judgment of our sin and made it possible for us to be counted as righteous before God, despite the depth and darkness of our trespasses (vv. 19, 21).

The names of Paul's gainsayers are buried in the dust of oblivion. They are part of the "old" that "has passed away" (v. 17). The new creation, however, is on the march. The word of reconciliation is celebrated in almost every town and village of our globe and the controlling love of Christ is still wooing millions to set aside their human prejudices and live for him.

GOSPEL: MARK 4:35–41

This story makes a transition from a cluster of parables (4:1–20, 21–25, 26–29, 30–34) to a chain of stories about miracles (4:35–41; 5:1–20, 21–23, 35–43, 24–34). Though the miracles are more dramatic than the parables and provoked both more amazement and more opposition, the purpose of the miracle stories is quite like that of the parables. Jesus' works in calming the storm, casting out demons, healing the sick, even raising the dead were not primarily acts of compassion, though his love was surely evident. Nor were they deeds of wonder like tricks of a magician designed to dazzle the crowds, though they often sparked amazement. They were rather signs that God was at work. As such they confirmed the messages of the parables.

The first major aim of our lesson stresses *the presence of the kingdom* (vv. 35–39). Its power—stirring while the farmer sleeps (vv.

26–29)—reaches to the sea itself and is available even while Jesus is slumbering (v. 38); its pervasiveness—promising vast and influential growth (vv. 30–32)—stretches to the winds and waves and makes them tame (vv. 39–41).

Where Jesus is present, there the kingdom is present. And his presence is more than sufficient to deal with Israel's ancient enemies, the sea and the wind. It was the desert wind that fatally tumbled the house of Job's children (Job 1:18–19). A sultry east wind teamed with the Assyrian sun to blast Jonah into submission (Jon. 4:8). Neither the wise man nor the prophet had the power to stay the assault of that enemy. But Jesus did. The blustery gusts that funneled down the Galilean hillsides and churned the water into frothy turbulence were no match for him.

Nor were the waves that beat fiercely in their eagerness to swamp the little boats. The same God who had rebuked the Sea of Reeds in Moses' day (Ps. 106:9) was on hand to speak stern commands to the Lake of Galilee and watch it turn to glass. The new exodus was on the way; the new creation was on the move. The Lord who will one day make all things new, when there is no more sea (Rev. 21:15), was showing beforehand what he has in mind and his power to accomplish it.

The presence of the kingdom prompted the second major point of our lesson—*the perplexity of the disciples* (vv. 40–41). It was one thing to reflect quietly on the mystery of the parables; it was another to be rocked first by the storm and then the majesty of this miracle.

The disciples had seen Jesus cast out demons and heal the sick (1:32–34), but for him to tackle the raw elements of nature was something else. Whether Jesus could prevail against the treachery of Galilean squalls they were not sure, but they knew that he was their only hope (v. 38). They called in fear more than faith, and Jesus' rebuke chided them.

Their final reaction to the quelling of the storm left them with questions more than answers: "Who then is this, that even wind and sea obey him?" (v. 41).

After all they were disciples not masters, pupils not teachers. They were witnesses to history's most amazing transition. They could not take it in all at once. But they were on their way. And their experience of perplexity gives us heart when we seem to learn slowly, while the presence of the kingdom—and the King—in the boat steadies us when the harsh winds beat and the waves climb high. Christian symbolism has often pictured the church as a boat; Christian faith has always known that Christ journeys with us, Master of wind and wave.

The Sixth Sunday After Pentecost

Lutheran	Roman Catholic	Episcopal	Pres/UCC/Chr	Meth/COCU
Lam. 3:22–33	Wisd. 1:13–15; 2:23–24	Deut. 15:7–11	Gen. 4:3–10	Lam. 3:22–33 or Wisd. 1:13–15; 2:23–24
2 Cor. 8:1–9, 13–14	2 Cor. 8:7–9, 13–15	2 Cor. 8:1–9, 13–15	2 Cor. 8:7–15	2 Cor. 8:1–15
Mark 5:21–24a, 35–43 or Mark 5:24b–34	Mark 5:21–43 or Mark 5:21–24, 35b–43	Mark 5:22–24, 35b–43	Mark 5:21–43	Mark 5:21–43

FIRST LESSON: LAMENTATIONS 3:22–33

Discovering this passage in this setting is like finding a diamond ring in an ash heap. The prevalent mood of Lamentations is funereal: the dominant sounds are wailing (1:2, 11, 16); the prominent sites are rubble (2:5, 8–9); the prescribed uniform is sackcloth (2:10).

The Jews had just experienced the worst event in their entire history prior to the Nazi holocaust. As Jeremiah had announced, Nebuchadnezzar's Babylonian troops, in 586 B.C., had ravaged Jerusalem and its environs, leveled and burned the Temple, and marched Judah's leaders to the Euphrates.

This *setting* meant that the calamity could only be lamented not avoided. It was too late for repentance or reform. Jerusalem had become a tattered widow, bereft of all she treasured by a Lord who had suddenly become an enemy (1:1; 2:4–5).

The *literary form* itself is designed to project the darkness of the scene. It is a dirge (*qīnāh* in Hebrew), funeral music composed of short, groaning lines, of dramatic contrasts, introduced by "How!" (1:1; 2:1; 4:1), that compares Judah's past glory with her present wretchedness, and of pleas for pity voiced by the broken city itself (1:9, 11–17).

Yet the poetry never deteriorates into a whine because it is held in check by an acrostic pattern. Each chapter, except chap. 5, leads us through the alphabet with each verse beginning with the next letter. The acrostic is not just an artistic curiosity. It also contributes to the meaning by symbolizing the completeness of the grief to which the lamenters gave expression: the calamity, their pain in it, and their remorse over it were voiced from *aleph* to *tau,* that is, from beginning to end, and four times over (chaps. 1—4).

The dirge, as a literary form, leaves no room for hope (cf. David's lament over the dead Saul and Jonathan; 2 Sam. 1:19–27). It is the language of the funeral chapel not the hospital room. To make room for hope, the literary form changes from dirge to complaint (Psalms 3; 22; 42; Job 10; Jer. 12:1–4; 15:15–18; 20:7–12). Complaints combine descriptions of suffering (Lam. 3:1–18) with pleas for help (3:19). Two other components contain the heart of the *message* of this lesson: declaration of trust (3:22–24) and instruction in wisdom (3:25–39).

The declaration of trust centers in *the constancy of the covenant God.* In the midst of his desolation the lone sufferer (note I, me, my; vv. 1–4) seems to reflect on the character and promises of God as he has heard them in the stories of Israel's past and in the prophecies of hope (Hos. 2:14–21; 14:1–7; Mic. 4:1–8; Jeremiah 30—31). And he begins to look beyond the rubble and to feel beyond the pain.

He finds comfort in God's attributes and actions: (1) acts of *steadfast love* (v. 22a) are the ways in which God helps his people because of his covenant grace; he keeps his part of the commitment though we have broken ours; (2) *mercies* (v. 22b) are the Lord's feelings of tender compassion toward his people as Shepherd, Father, Husband; (3) *faithfulness* (v. 23) is the total reliability of God to keep his promises and achieve his purposes.

The sufferer also takes courage from the availability of God. He calls the Lord his *portion* (v. 24), borrowing language from the allotting of the land when the tribes settled in Canaan (Josh. 18:5ff.). As the tribal territory was available to house and sustain its inhabitants, so the Lord can be depended on to provide for his own.

Then, the plaintiff turns instructor, expounding *the purposes of human suffering.* His breakthrough from despair qualifies him to share his insights with others: (1) patient waiting for divine rescue brings unexpected benefits in maturity (vv. 25–27); (2) believing this will enable us to bear otherwise intolerable injury (vv. 28–30); (3) trusting in the covenant loyalty of God will remind us that his ultimate goal, even where judgment is necessary, is salvation (vv. 31–33).

The tone of lament and complaint continues to the close of the book. The land remains in ruins; the people in mourning. But for one bright moment the nature and purposes of God have been perceived. And that perception, the diamond in the ashheap, is enough to see them and us through whatever suffering comes our way.

SECOND LESSON: 2 CORINTHIANS 8:1–9, 13–14

In this letter, Paul has (1) defended his apostleship (chaps. 1—5), (2) urged the Corinthians to exercise spiritual discipline (chap. 6), and (3) commended them for the change of heart (chap. 7). Here he comes to one of his chief purposes—his desire that the Corinthians contribute to the collections which the gentile churches were receiving for the mother congregation in Jerusalem (cf. 1 Cor. 16:1–4). Christian generosity, then, is the nub of what Paul stresses here.

In stating *the motivation for generosity,* he brushes aside heart-rending descriptions of human need based on the severity of the famine in A.D. 46–47 when Claudius was emperor (Acts 11:27–30). He bypasses appeal to the special status of Jerusalem Christians. Instead he recites the ways in which God's grace has been demonstrated.

First, God's grace had prompted the Macedonians (at Philippi, Thessalonica, Beroea, Acts 16—17) to extraordinary generosity despite their harsh experiences of persecution and poverty (vv. 1–2). The badges of their benevolence were several: they gave more than they could afford (v. 3); they begged for the opportunity to share (v. 4); they gave lavishly of their time, interest, and energy to the Lord and to Paul (v. 5). Grace has been comprehended when grace is extended to others.

Second, God's grace had equipped the Corinthians for all kinds of spiritual service (v. 7). Firm faith in Christ, ability to persuade others to believe, wisdom to apply divine truth, zeal to keep serving, and love for the apostles who disciplined them—these assets marked the spiritual excellence of Paul's hearers. All these graces called for one more to complete their ministry—the grace of charity (*charis* is the word), of openhanded giving.

Finally, God's grace was expressed magnificently in Christ's incarnation which Paul pictures as an exchange of wealth for poverty (v. 9), a surrender of the glories of heavenly fellowship for the cabining limitations of life in human flesh (cf. John 1:1, 14). Yet out of that poverty came the vast wealth of our knowing God and being at peace with him through Jesus Christ. At the heart of grace lies great giving. Jesus proved that.

Paul's word on *the administration of generosity* deserves a brief comment (v. 6). Though we do not know the precise role Titus played in the collection—perhaps he had helped the Corinthians to prepare for it on a visit a year earlier (9:2)—it is likely that Paul was counting on him to organize, supervise, and transport the funds. It is enough to note that using Titus's administrative skills in no way detracted from the "gracious work" of the offering. It is part of divine grace to use human stewards to enable others to do works of grace.

Paul's final thought touches on *the consequences of generosity* (vv. 13–14). The key is "equality" (v. 14). Not that everybody would have the same amount of food, wealth, or goods, but that, in the ups and downs of economic and agricultural cycles, those who had more at any one time (in this case, the Corinthians) would help those in present want (here, the Jerusalem Christians). On another occasion circumstances might be reversed, hence, the equality of each church helping the other in time of need. The argument is clinched by the illustration of the exodus manna: "He that gathered much had nothing over, and he that gathered little had no lack" (Exod. 16:15–18).

The combination of theological insights with the motivation for stewardship and practical suggestions for its implementation is Paul at his best. Along with all else that he did well, he was a pastor's pastor.

GOSPEL: MARK 5:21–24a, 35–43

Mark stitches together story after story to make his point: The kingdom is here in the person of Jesus of Nazareth, who is teacher and so much more, prophet and so much more. Lord of sea, wind, and storm Jesus has shown himself to be (4:35–41), and Lord over demonic powers even in gentile territory (5:1–20). Our lesson brings Jesus back to Jewish terrain (v. 21) and illustrates his lordship in an ultimate miracle—he raises Jairus's daughter from the dead.

Mark's account pictures *a lordship expressed in compassion*. Jesus leaves the crowd and goes with Jairus to intervene in the mortal illness of Jairus's little daughter (vv. 22–24). We hear no conversation, only the Jewish leader's desperate need followed by the terse yet eloquent, "And he went away with him" (v. 24). Other clues to the compassion are found in the tenderness with which he deals with the little girl, addressing her with affection (v. 41) and calling attention to her need for food (v. 43).

The story also portrays *a lordship demonstrated in power*. Jesus went with Jairus in full confidence that he could stay a fatal illness and brushed aside the reports of the girl's death, "Do not fear, only believe" (vv. 35–36). Moreover, he rebuked the noisy mourners and evoked their scorn with, "The child is not dead but sleeping" (v. 39). The New Testament often salutes Jesus' resurrection power by branding death as sleep (1 Cor. 15:51; 1 Thess. 4:13). The clearest signal of his powerful lordship was the amazing ease with which he touched and called the girl back to life (vv. 41–42).

Mark has carefully built his accounts of Jesus' invincible power to a climax in this miracle. Exorcism of the unclean spirit (1:21–28), healing of Simon's feverish mother-in-law (1:29–31), summary statements of healing activity (1:32–39), cleansing of the leper (1:40–45), restoration of the paralytic (2:1–12), straightening of the withered hand (3:1–6), silencing of the storm (4:35–41), deliverance of the Gerasene demoniac (5:1–20), healing of the woman's hemorrhage (5:25–34; note this as another example of Mark's skill at tucking a second story into the heart of another narrative)—these magnificent displays of power are all outdone by the resurrection of Jairus's daughter. Here the last enemy, death (1 Cor. 15:26), has begun to be destroyed. The messianic kingdom is built with resurrection power, and Mark uses the story of Jairus's daughter as part of the preparation for Jesus' resurrection, with which his Gospel may have concluded in its earliest form (16:1–8).

The context suggests that Mark is pointing to *a lordship destined for conflict*. The next paragraph announces the offense taken by Jesus' countrymen (6:3) and their unbelief (6:6). Many details in the lesson contribute to our sense of that conflict: (1) it is not a wild Gentile but a distinguished leader of the synagogue, elected by his fellow worshipers, who believes that Jesus will heal; (2) the two miracles involve persons who would have had little standing in the community and would have been considered unworthy of the time of most rabbis—an ailing woman and a little girl; (3) both persons would have been deemed unfit, even contaminating, to touch—one hemorrhaging (cf. Lev. 15:25–30), the other dead (cf. Lev. 21:1–5; 22:4–7); (4) the repetition of the number twelve (the woman sick twelve years, v. 25; the maiden twelve years old, v. 42) may be more than a coincidence—an oblique attack on Israel's spiritual impotence, a furtive reference to the twelve tribes. Conflict smoldered, then in Jesus' home, burst into full flame. The resurrection fueled the fires of skepticism, despite all Jesus' efforts to hush the matter (v. 43). A lordship so demanding, backed by wonders so mind-boggling, put to the test the faith of all who heard.

By all this Mark reminds us of *a lordship apprehended by faith.* Jairus declared his faith by coming to Jesus (v. 23). The woman demonstrated hers by reaching out to touch his garments and then confessing what she had done (v. 28, 33–34). Jesus urged Jairus, in the face of the fatal report, to stop being afraid, and continue to trust (v. 36). The power and grace of the kingdom were not available to human endeavors, nor to religious ritual, nor to magical actions (note how unlike a magician mumbling mystic words or practicing in secret is Jesus' approach to the healings), but to faith alone.

The Seventh Sunday After Pentecost

Lutheran	Roman Catholic	Episcopal	Pres/UCC/Chr	Meth/COCU
Ezek. 2:1–5	Ezek. 2:2–5	Ezek. 2:1–7	Ezek. 2:1–5	Ezek. 2:1–7
2 Cor. 12:7–10	2 Cor. 12:7–10	2 Cor. 12:2–10	2 Cor. 12:7–10	2 Cor. 12:7–10
Mark 6:1–6	Mark 6:1–6	Mark 6:1–6	Mark 6:1–6	Mark 6:1–6

FIRST LESSON: EZEKIEL 2:1–5

The dazzling vision of the universal sovereignty of God and the glories of his throne above the firmament (1:4–28a) had left Ezekiel flat on his face, overcome by awe, seeking relief from its brilliance (1:28b). The vision was the first stage in the prophet's commissioning which, he tells us, took place when the hand of the Lord was on him, as he lived with other exiles by the Chebar, a channel of the Euphrates southeast of Babylon. The year was 594 B.C.

As impressive as the vision was—with its four-faced, four-winged living creatures, wheels within wheels, crystal firmament, rainbow brightness around the sapphire throne—it said nothing specific to Ezekiel beyond the overwhelming aura of majesty which prostrated the prophet. He had heard no intelligible sounds, only the roar of beating wings (1:24) and a mysterious voice from above the firmament (1:25).

The contrast between all that and the plain speech of our lesson contributes powerfully to the flow of Ezekiel's book. The call-vision of chap. 1 with its fascinating, almost surrealistic, imagery is followed by the very clear auditions of 2:1—3:15. What Ezekiel saw and puzzled at gave him perspective to carry out the assignments mandated by God. The direct call-announcements made Ezekiel a captive not so much to the Babylonian conquerors as to the divine word.

The gist of our lesson can best be grasped from the various formulas that God uses to enlist Ezekiel as a prophet. By lineage a priest (1:3), Ezekiel was at the age when priestly duties usually began—thirty (1:1)—yet unable to practice them in a strange land, cut off from the shelter of the Temple with its tangible expressions of Israel's religious life. But God had other plans for him and step by step unfolded them.

The lesson begins with *the call to attention* (vv. 1–2). The address to Ezekiel is significant and recurs nearly a hundred times throughout the book—son of man. Mere mortal or representative human being seems to be its meaning. It marks Ezekiel off from the lofty mysteries of the heavenly vision and plants his feet firmly on the ground. His tasks will center in human problems, and, to carry them out, he will be in constant need of divine resources. This is made clear by the fact that Ezekiel rises only when the Spirit enters him and stands him up. The God who, to get Ezekiel's attention, gave the command also supplied the power to obey that command.

Next the Lord lays on his servant *the commission to speak* (vv. 3–4a). Again reminding him of his human frailty (son of man), God sets down the most direct kind of order, "I send you to the people of Israel, to a nation of rebels." The difficulty of the assignment is tipped off by the terms used to describe Israel: rebels who revolt against me as King and the terms of my covenant, who refuse to behave as loyal vassals (transgressors), who are hard-faced in their impudence, and tough-hearted in their stubbornness. No wonder God sent the dazzling vision as preparation for a ministry to such a people.

The summary of *the content of the message* could not have been briefer (v. 4b). It is the formula with which prophetic speeches—especially judgment speeches—frequently begin: "Thus says the Lord God." This is called messenger formula, and its background in the life and culture of Israel can be seen in the account of Jacob's messengers sent to Esau (Gen. 32:3–5). In Ezekiel's commissioning, without dropping a clue as to the specifics of the message, it makes two points: (1) the prophet speaks not on his own but as a divinely dispatched messenger; (2) the Lord is present with his people in the person of the prophet to declare his word and will to them.

The final verse makes this latter point clear in its use of a familiar formula: "They will know that there has been a prophet among them" (v. 5). This formula—a favorite of Ezekiel's—is called the proof or recognition formula. Here it features *the recognition of God's presence* in and through the prophet. This recognition that God is there speaking to them, that he has not abandoned them and they must reckon with him, is crucial whether or not the people obey ("hear") God's word.

The chain of revelation cannot be broken by exile, nor by the sin that led to exile. The Lord God of Israel is as much at home by the Chebar as in Jerusalem. The One who sent prophets like Jeremiah to try to head off calamity has now commissioned Ezekiel to explain it to them, help them cope with it, and point them beyond it. But more important than anything specific the prophet will say is the fact that he is there. And with him he brings the word of God.

SECOND LESSON: 2 CORINTHIANS 12:7–10

Like Ezekiel, Paul was a witness to the heavenly mysteries of God's presence. Unlike Ezekiel, Paul thought it best not to describe what he had seen (12:1–6). His handling of the situation called for delicacy: his experience of visions and revelations was part of his apostolic authority—he had a more intimate knowledge of the heavenly realities than any of his opponents who boasted of superior knowledge; yet what he had heard was so much a part of the world to come that he dared not utter it to earthly ears. As a messenger, his aware-

ness of God's ministry had been sharpened and his confidence in
God's sovereignty strengthened—and all this early in his ministry
("fourteen years ago," v. 2)—but his message itself could not include
what he had seen and heard.

"Elation" is what he calls the experience, elation so exhilarating
that it has to be kept in check (v. 7). And a compensating somberness is
introduced into his life by a thorn of suffering. More than anything
else what he learned from all this was a sense of apostolic dependence.
The person commissioned to carry the saving word was never inde-
pendent of the Savior who sent him. The call, the message, the power,
the safety, the success of the messenger were all gifts of God's grace.

This sense of dependence Paul learned at the cost of high frustration, begging Christ three times to provide relief (v. 8)—one of the few
recorded instances where Paul prayed directly to Jesus (cf. 1 Cor.
16:22). Yet out of Christ's refusal to answer that prayer came a
strengthened character, a deepened faith, and, to those outsiders wise
enough to perceive, a heightened credibility.

For one thing, Paul learned *humility in spite of revelations* (v. 7).
The textbook for this lesson was a harsh one, some sort of infliction
with which God allowed Satan to prick Paul (cf. Job 1—2). Was it
physical? The theories are many: an eye ailment (Gal. 4:15), neuras-
thenia, malaria, epilepsy. However, Acts and the Epistles also contain ample evidence of the apostle's rugged durability. If we interpret
flesh in less physical terms, then the thorn may be some bout with
doubt or despair or a specific blow of ridicule or persecution, as the list
of hardships in v. 10 may point to. Whatever the thorn may have been,
God used it for the good of Paul's character and mission, as it goaded
him to trust God and get on with his work.

Paul also learned about *power in the face of weakness* (v. 9).
Stronger than the sting of the thorn was the assurance of the Christ.
Frustration became the context for grace; life at the end of our tether is
the setting for Christ's mighty care—note how strong a word "grace"
is in this passage, virtually synonymous with power. No thorn can
inflict more than the loving commitment of Christ to us can assuage.
As quinine shows its power best when malaria has weakened us most,
as cortisone tackles iritis just when it is most painful, so Christ's
gracious power, Christ's powerful grace, does its finest work when all
else that we depend on has been knocked aside.

Paul's final lesson in dependence had to do with *contentment in the midst of calamity* (v. 10). The Greek word may be even stronger, "delight," which goes beyond contentment. None of us would call such a list of experiences delightful—weaknesses (or illnesses), insults (or acts of insolent arrogance), hardships (perhaps torture,), persecutions (usually for religious reasons), and calamities (intense pressure with little room for escape). Yet Paul does. Not because his values are masochistic, but because they are straight. If all of this is for Christ's sake, then Christ's power is available to help us survive, to build up our faith, and to extend the kingdom.

What a chain of providence this is! What a testimony to the mystery of God's way! A vision too grand to repeat leads to a suffering too grave to bear which in turn leads to a grace too powerful to do without which then leads to a delight too puzzling to comprehend. Incredible? Yes, but for the fact that Christ is there at every point, and his presence makes the whole experience sensible.

GOSPEL: MARK 6:1–6

In the heart of the Pentecost season we find a lesson preparing us for Lent. At heart, Mark, like the other Gospels, is a passion story. Its climax is the betrayal, trial, death, and resurrection of Jesus. And much of what Mark records along the way is designed to ready his readers for that climax. The rejection at Nazareth—we infer that this was the setting from the mention of "his own country" (v. 1) and his family as "here with us" (v. 3)—is an event toward the beginning of his mission that sets the stage for the rejection in Jerusalem at the end.

The brief paragraph is artfully crafted. It begins with his countrymen's astonishment at Jesus' miracles; when it closes, the miracles have ceased and Jesus is marveling at their unbelief. The movement from their reaction to his frames the outline of the lesson.

The initial astonishment of the friends is expressed when Jesus, as prominent visitors were permitted to do, "began to teach in the synagogue" (v. 2). His hearers put together the compelling wisdom with which he taught about God and the reports of the chain of miracles that Mark has recounted, peaking at the resurrection of Jairus's daughter (5:41–43), and posed to each other the puzzling question: Where did this man get all this? The quality of the teaching spoke for itself; so did the power of the miracles. Yet they knew his roots and found in them no way to account for his uniqueness.

This puzzlement led them to pose *the crucial question:* "This man is the carpenter; isn't he (the Greek word for *not* calls for a "yes" answer) the son of Mary?" (v. 3). The jabs at Jesus' credentials are a one-two punch: (1) his craft—only here is he called a carpenter, literally a craftsman—would have given him no preparation for his ministry; (2) the description, Mary's son, with no mention of Joseph, seems to have been a not-so-subtle way of branding him as illegitimate. Then the whole argument for his commonness was buttressed in the mention by name of his brothers (which could also mean cousins or other near male relatives) and the reference to his sisters. It was as if they all seconded Nathaniel's question: "Can anything good come out of Nazareth?" (John 1:46). And for some foolish reason the question of roots outweighed the demonstration of fruits which had so astounded them. They were literally tripped up ("took offense" means "stumbled," v. 3).

Then it was Jesus' turn to speak and he commented on their question, as any wise man might, with *the crucial proverb:* honor for a prophet everywhere but among his own people (v. 4). He makes no effort to defend his unique role in the kingdom; no proof of his messiahship rushes from his lips. He does, however, acknowledge his prophetic office and reminds them, if they are wise enough to catch on, of their long history of rejecting prophets (Amos 2:11–12).

The response of his countrymen, then, was no surprise to Jesus, though Mark did register *the final wonderment* (v. 6), which was the Master's reaction, wonderment at their disbelief. How different they were from the woman with the hemorrhage whose faith made her well (5:34), how different from Jairus who stopped fearing and continued to trust even when his friends said, "She's dead" (5:35–36). Strangers reached out to touch; townspersons turned their backs.

And Jesus, with a few compassionate exceptions (v. 5), went elsewhere to spread good news and do good works. But the future is clear. The rejection at Nazareth will be duplicated elsewhere, especially at Jerusalem. The wonder of the incarnation was too great for all but a few to grasp. The distance that God bridged in becoming man was so vast, the servant form in which he sent his Messiah was so veiled, that even those closest to the event, especially those closest, missed its meaning. Pentecost is the right season for us to study this. Through the gift of the Spirit we can say what the Nazarenes did not: "We believe; Lord, help our unbelief."

The Eighth Sunday After Pentecost

Lutheran	Roman Catholic	Episcopal	Pres/UCC/Chr	Meth/COCU
Amos 7:10–15	Amos 7:12–15	Amos 7:7–15	Amos 7:12–17	Amos 7:7–17
Eph. 1:3–14	Eph. 1:3–14 or Eph. 1:3–10	Eph. 1:1–14	Eph. 1:3–10	Eph. 1:1–14
Mark 6:7–13	Mark 6:7–13	Mark 6:7–13	Mark 6:7–13	Mark 6:7–13

FIRST LESSON: AMOS 7:10–15

We have no narrative to describe Amos's call to be a prophet—nothing like the detailed accounts of what happened to Isaiah (chap. 6), Jeremiah (chap. 1), and Ezekiel (1:1—3:15). What we do have is Amos's strong conviction that the Lord commissioned him, a conviction put to the test by the fiercest opposition possible: the royal court and the official priesthood. This passage condenses into a brief report many of the monumental issues of biblical discipleship when it encounters entrenched and hostile authority.

Amaziah's complaint to Jeroboam II (793–753 B.C.) begins the report (vv. 10–11). The complaint has two parts: (1) the priest's summary indictment of Amos's conspiracy (v. 10); (2) the direct evidence to support the charge in Amos's own words, announcing Jeroboam's death and Israel's exile (v. 11).

In Amaziah's charges we find the reason for the placement of this report, interrupting the series of five visions of judgment that dominate the text from 7:1 to 9:4. Vision three, the plumbline that exposed Israel's crookedness, contains a direct threat against the sanctuaries or shrines of Israel and the royal household (7:9). And announcements of attack and exile are spotted strategically throughout the text (2:13–16; 3:11–15; 4:1–3; 5:1–2; 6:7, 14). Amaziah's complaint was well documented in Amos's speeches. What was unusual was the implication of all of this: *the prophet was a traitor,* threatening, by the power of his words, the very existence of the political and religious systems that held the Northern Kingdom together.

Amaziah's command to Amos (vv. 12–13) may have come on his own initiative or at the direction of the king. News could travel from Bethel to Samaria (about fifty kilometers) and back in two or three days. The command is specific and comprehensive: go back to Judah (v. 12); never again prophesy here (v. 13). The brief clauses—we can hear Amaziah spitting them out between his teeth: "Eat bread there," "Prophesy there" (in Judah where you came from)—expose the center of the conflict. Amaziah assumed that Amos was a professional prophet who moved north to carpetbag, earn his living (bread), and ply his trade (prophesying).

Amaziah saw the issue as an unwanted invasion of a royal sanctuary by an ambitious itinerant prophet. As Jerusalem was literally a royal city whose temple was owned and maintained by Solomon and his successors, so Bethel's shrine was directly sponsored by Jeroboam. *This sanctuary is the king's precinct,* was the essence of Amaziah's explanation. It was open only to those whom the king and his staff allowed to frequent it.

Amos's explanation to Amaziah pinpointed the issue (vv. 14–15). The prophet did not quibble over the priest's paraphrase of his message, nor deny uttering the threats attributed to him, nor protest about being misquoted. Amos's reply was that Amaziah had totally misunderstood his motivation. He came not as a professional prophet nor a member of a prophetic guild (compare Elisha's "sons"; 1 Kings 20:35; 2 Kings 2:3ff.). Raising animals and growing fruit were Amos's legitimate occupations. He was in no way dependent on prophesying for a livelihood. If the priest and the king he served had a quarrel, *their quarrel was with God not the prophet.*

Amos was only following orders. He could no more disobey God's command to prophesy than a farm boy could hear a lion roar and not be frightened (3:8). Besides, the question of who owned the shrine of Bethel was irrelevant. The people of Israel were God's people. God, not the hierarchy, had the right to determine who spoke to them and what was said.

To bar God's word from Bethel was irony indeed. The place had gained its name and reputation from the Lord's revelation there to Israel's esteemed ancestor (Gen. 28:10–17). Amaziah's opposition was exhibit A for Amos's accusation that rejecting prophets was one of the most heinous of all sins—a blatant spurning of God's grace (2:11–12), for which Amaziah was to pay a terrible price (7:16–17).

This lesson is a remarkable picture of courage born of conviction. But the core of its word to us is not Amos's boldness but God's sovereignty. All life's structures whether political or religious are dependent on his grace and subject to this judgment. True is the prophet who proclaims this, and wise are the people who hear.

SECOND LESSON: EPHESIANS 1:3–14

In one Greek sentence of over two hundred words Paul has compressed some of the loftiest expressions of divine purpose and human destiny to be found anywhere in world literature. Each clause is freighted with profound significance and the entire paragraph is alight with celebration, from the blessing with which it begins to the praise of his glory with which it ends.

The centrality of Christ is one of its controlling themes. Phrases like "in him" and "through him" dot the sentence, so that all God does—in choosing us (v. 4), destining us to be his children (v. 5), bestowing grace and redemption on us (vv. 6–7), achieving his purposes of uniting all things (vv. 9–10), calling us to live for his praise (v. 12), and sealing us with the Holy Spirit (v. 13)—he does in connection with Christ. Let any one who wants to know what Christ means to Christian faith and life ponder this passage.

At the same time, this Christocentric melody comes with a trinitarian accompaniment. It is the Father who is first blessed (v. 3) and who is responsible for the garland of spiritual blessing described here so floridly. And it is the Holy Spirit who is the guarantee that everything promised by God will ultimately be possessed by his people (vv. 13–14). Let anyone who wants to understand the ministry of the blessed Trinity begin by reflecting on Paul's outburst of praise.

The certainty of God's will is another controlling theme. What God has purposed he is achieving. Like a drumbeat this theme sets the rhythm of the passage. The *scope* of his will embraces the whole of time from "before the foundation of the world" until the "fulness of the times" (v. 10), which begins with Christ's advent, and unto the end of the age when we enter into the inheritance he has planned for us (v. 14).

The *range* of his will is nothing less than "all things" both in heaven and on earth (v. 10). God will not rest content until all that he had in mind when he spoke creation into being and planted humankind on this spinning sphere has been brought to fruition (v. 11). His aim is to restore harmony to the universe, which has for ages been at odds with itself through human rebellion, by bringing everything together (the Greek is literally "heading up" or "summing up") in Christ (v. 10).

The *centerpiece* of this will is the church, chosen to be holy and blameless (v. 4), bearing God's own stamp of ownership which is the Holy Spirit (v. 13). Human beings threw the universe out of kilter by rejecting God's lordship. God himself is seeing to it that human beings, his church, surrender to that lordship as the crucial step in setting things right.

The surety of God's grace, the third controlling theme, is what makes all this possible. The text radiates *love,* love of the Father for us which is a prime motive for the whole plan (v. 5), and his love for Christ, the beloved (v. 6), which forms the context for redemption and forgiveness (v. 7), without which the ultimate reconciliation of all things would not take place. Divine *initiative* permeates the text as another expression of grace. God is the subject of all the key verbs. Where "we" becomes the subject it is always in response to the overtures of divine grace. *Generosity* abounds in this sentence, which uses language that would be deemed extravagant in any other setting: "every spiritual blessing" (v. 3), "glorious grace . . . freely bestowed" (v. 6), "riches of his grace . . . lavished upon us" (vv. 7–8), "all wisdom and insight" (v. 9).

Truth is a seamless garment. Perhaps that is why Paul pressed so much into one sentence. He knew that everything that God does is connected to everything else and that where each person of the Trinity ministers the whole Godhead is involved. We have to break the lesson into its component themes to grasp its several nuances. Then we need to let it stand whole again and join with Paul in the blessing and praise.

GOSPEL: MARK 6:7–13

Jesus' response to the rejection of his ministry was to extend it. Twice in Mark we see that. Once, when the Pharisees and Herodians plotted to destroy him after he had healed the withered hand in the synagogue on the Sabbath (3:1–6), he took his disciples, ministered to vast crowds from every part of the land, and appointed the Twelve to be his special co-workers (3:7–19). Again, in our lesson, the staggering unbelief of Jesus' countrymen in Nazareth (6:1–6a) has led to an extension of his efforts throughout the land. He himself continued his ministry in the villages. But instead of taking his disciples with him, he sent them on their own to carry out the work.

The rejection led to *an intensification of the mission.* By dividing the team into six pairs, Jesus greatly accelerated the pace at which the news of the kingdom could be brought to the various towns and villages. *Urgency* seems to be a prevailing mood: they were to travel light (vv. 8–9) and stay only where they were welcome (v. 11). The mention of staff and sandals may echo the passover instructions (Exod. 12:11) with their note of urgency—the readiness to be on the move when God summons. In both stories, the redemption of God's people was at hand; they had to be able to pull up stakes at a moment's notice.

The intensification was marked by *simplicity* as well as urgency. The contrast between the urgent austerity of the disciples' life (they were not to move to better quarters even if opportunity were afforded, v. 10) and the corrupt opulence of Herod's court is intentional (6:14–29)—another example of a story wrapped within a story, since the account of the disciples' mission actually closes at v. 30 when they report to Jesus the results of their labors. While Herod had bevies of servants at his beck, Jesus' men were utterly dependent on the generosity and hospitality of others.

In all of this strategy to blanket the countryside with word of the gospel, Jesus is planning *a transition in ministry.* Twice rejected already in Mark's account, he sensed that the time would come when he no longer would be able to lead the mission. Its continuity depended on the work of others. Those whom he had personally taught and who had traveled with him were to be the core of the group charged with carrying out the commission of Christ. The church was about to be born. Its future leaders were being trained as interns.

The need for transition is sharpened by Herod's treatment of John the Baptist. The cruel decapitation of the great forerunner became an implicit prophecy of Jesus' own death, toward which Mark's record is relentlessly leading us. The intensity of the mission contributed to this need for transition: the spreading word of the kingdom and its power (v. 13) seemed to spark within Herod the same antipathy toward Jesus that had sent John to his early death (vv. 14–16).

Finally, the sending of the Twelve was *a demonstration of the kingdom.* Among other things, the exorcisms and healings effected by the disciples proved that Jesus was not a magician accomplishing his works by secret rituals nor a charlatan deceiving the multitudes by illusive trickery. His own followers—fisherfolk and tax-collectors—could do the same thing. Perhaps it was not so incredible that a carpenter from Nazareth (v. 3), a familiar neighbor, could do the works of God, could be a prophet, and much more.

In fact the language of Mark suggests that the disciples themselves took on a prophetic function: (1) they were to shake the dust from their feet as a testimony against the town that rejected them (v. 4); (2) they used olive oil to anoint the sick (v. 13). Both of these practices seem to be symbolic acts which express God's judgment and grace respectively. The simplicity of the gear with which they traveled may possibly be viewed in the same way—an expression of the seriousness of the kingdom and its demand of total dedication. Background for such acts can be found in Isaiah (e.g., 20:1–6), Jeremiah (e.g., 13:1–11; 27:1–11), and Ezekiel (e.g., chaps. 4—5), where God commands a prophet to act out a message not just to speak it.

Nazareth had not honored Jesus as prophet (v. 4). Jesus, in turn, filled the countryside with prophets who spoke the word and performed the works of the kingdom.

The Ninth Sunday After Pentecost

Lutheran	Roman Catholic	Episcopal	Pres/UCC/Chr	Meth/COCU
Jer. 23:1–6	Jer. 23:1–6	Isa. 57:14b–21	Jer. 23:1–6	Jer. 23:1–6
Eph. 2:13–22	Eph. 2:13–18	Eph. 2:11–22	Eph. 2:11–18	Eph. 2:11–22
Mark 6:30–34	Mark 6:30–34	Mark 6:30–44	Mark 6:30–34	Mark 6:30–44

FIRST LESSON: JEREMIAH 23:1–6

More often than not the prophets concentrated on the failure of leadership in Israel. As conscious as they were of the corruption of the entire land, they gave unusual attention to the persons responsible for the religious, moral, social, and political character of life—

priests, prophets, wise men, and kings. And especially the kings, whose duty was to integrate every facet of life under the covenant that the Lord had made with the people (cf. Ps. 72; 89:19–37).

The context of our lesson makes all of this clear. It details the responsibilities of the true sons of David (22:1–4), spells out the consequence of shirking these duties (22:5–10), and ushers several of Judah's last kings before the divine bench to hear their judgment: Shallum (i.e., Jehoahaz, 609 B.C.; 22:11–12), Jehoiakim (609–598 B.C.; 22:13–19), Coniah (i.e., Jehoiachin, 598–597 B.C.; 22:24–30).

Jeremiah sums up God's verdict in a brief judgment speech that takes the form of a woe oracle (23:1–2) which, as usual (cf. Isa. 5:8–25; Hab. 2:6–19), warns that our sin will find us out, that the harm we have done to others will boomerang against us. But then the judge turns savior (the two terms are closely connected in biblical thought) and switches from woe-oracle to salvation speech (vv. 3–6) as a reminder that he, not the kings, is the ultimate keeper of the covenant.

The failure of the false shepherds is that they destroyed and scattered the sheep (v. 1). Tolerant of oppression at home and stupid in politics abroad, they let injustice thrive, formed alliances with the impotent Egyptians, and refused to trust God to help them in their dealings with Nebuchadnezzar's Babylonians (21:1–14). And all of this in violation of the well-known requirements for shepherding that Ezekiel later listed (34:1–6). The selfish, stubborn corruption of a whole line of kings will receive its deserved reward: the kingship itself will be cut off by captivity in Babylon.

None of this means, however, that God is through with the sheep. *The rescue of the scattered flock* is the promise that begins the salvation-speech (v. 3). They are a remnant—a tattered vestige of their former glory, weakened by warfare, slavery, and exile—yet in God's grace they are a new beginning. When he shepherds them again to their fold, their fertility will be astounding. The full impact of the judgment will be reversed, and they will be poised on the edge of better days.

New shepherds are vital to such rescue and are part of the promise (v. 4). From all that they suffered before in terror, confusion, and harm, the people of Judah will then be freed. The word of the Lord will guarantee it.

The picture of salvation is brought to its climax not in the general promise of good leadership but in the specific announcement of *the choosing of the true shepherd* (vv. 5–6). The new king will have the *right credentials:* he comes from the right family, fulfills the promise of continuity contained in the covenant with David (2 Samuel 7), and is the true heir to David's righteous leadership (for Branch, see Isa. 11:1; Zech. 6:12; the idea is that the Davidic tree, though cut back by destruction and exile, is not dead, since God has promised to keep it alive).

The new king will also perform the *right duties,* ruling wisely, enforcing in the whole community the justice and righteousness that the covenant demands (v. 5), and providing full rescue and total security for both halves of the severed kingdom (v. 6).

This magnificent combination of lineage and performance is summed up in the *right name* given to the king: "The Lord is our righteousness" (v. 6). We should understand righteousness here as referring not only to the perfection of God's character which by grace he shares with his people as they worship and obey him but also to the marvelous way in which he vindicates and saves those who pledge full loyalty to him.

The point is clear: behind the true shepherd who will reign in David's stead stands the great Shepherd who supplies all the lacks of his people. Zedekiah (597–586 B.C.), Judah's last king, bore a name that should have carried such a message—the Lord is righteous. But his conduct belied the meaning. Nothing less than a new and greater king with a new and greater name would meet both the people's needs and the Lord's demands.

SECOND LESSON: EPHESIANS 2:13–22

Ephesians begins with a medley of hymns: a hymn that celebrates the eternal plan of God and the role of the church in it (1:3–14), a hymn rejoicing in the resurrection and all it accomplished (1:20–23), a hymn treasuring God's grace (2:4–7), and a hymn commemorating the power of the cross to make peace between Jew and Gentile (2:14–18). If it is true creeds were meant to be sung not recited, we would best appreciate these if we could set them to music.

Whether recited or chanted they are one of Scripture's grand anthems. *How Christ makes peace* is the major theme. The hymn enumerates the ways in which Christ was personally involved through his death: (1) "in the blood of Christ" (v. 13) marks sacrifice as a key component in the transaction; Christ is the willing victim through whose death Jew and Gentile were brought together; (2) "in his flesh"

(v. 15) is another way of saying the same thing; the law that loomed like a barrier between Jew and Gentile no longer need separate them, because Christ had fulfilled it for both Jew and Gentile in his own life and had borne the judgment for their failure to keep it in his own flesh; a whole new way of relating to God was open to both Jew and Gentile; (3) that way was possible "in one body" (v. 16); only in the person of Christ stretched out for our sin did the new possibility come into being—that Jew and Gentile could be one; (4) "through the cross" (v. 16) clinches the emphasis on Christ's death as the ground of the new thing being done—a new thing so drastic that only the Messiah could accomplish it and that only at the price of his own life.

But Christ is initiator as well as victim, priest as well as sacrifice: (1) he makes both one by breaking down the walls that separate, as though he who once cleansed the temple now redesigns it by tearing down the wall that blocked gentile access to the heart of worship (v. 14); (2) he creates "in himself one new man in place of the two" (v. 15), not forming a hybrid Jew-Gentile, like an Afro-American or a Eur-Asian, but bringing into being something new—a body of Christians, a church, which is not a Jewish-Gentile mixture but a whole new entity marked by its present oneness—a oneness that was not its former history; (3) he did all this by reconciling us both to God at the same time he reconciled us to each other (v. 16).

Scarcely anything shows the centrality of Christ more than his reconciling role here. This is a role otherwise ascribed to God in Paul's parlance (2 Cor. 5:19).

In all of this, hostility or enmity was the condition to be dealt with. The temple wall was its human expression (v. 15): Jews and Gentiles not only differed in language, culture, and religious practice, but they actually hated each other. The Gentiles are pictured as utter outsiders—separated, alienated, strangers, hopeless, and godless (v. 12), as far away from Israel as could be (v. 13).

Yet Jews, whatever advantage they had over the Gentiles as children of promise and covenant, also had hostility to face—not only their hostility to the pagans but God's hostility toward them. This too Christ ended (v. 16).

And in their common reconciliation to God, whom each group in its own way had offended, they found their new oneness as they heard Christ's word of peace, preached with equal cause and equal results to those near (the Jews) and those far off (the Gentiles, v. 17). All this reconciliation, all this quelling of hostility, is so intimately connected with Christ's person and work that he is our peace personified (v. 14), the beautiful fulfillment of Isaiah's prophecy (9:6), the true embodiment of his own beatitude (Matt. 5:9).

What Christ's peace brings is the note with which the lesson closes (2:18–22). *Access* to God through the Spirit is one gift of that peace. Pagan rites were never an acceptable route to the biblical God; the Temple and the law, the traditional Jewish way, have been replaced by a new and living Road (Heb. 10:20) so that both may worship God in spirit and truth (John 4:24). Jews do not become Gentiles in order to worship, nor Gentiles Jews. Both come together through the Holy Spirit who dwells within them by faith in Christ.

Fellowship with each other is the second gift. Jews and Gentiles who previously lived in separate areas of a town and who could not sit at table with each other are now "fellow citizens and members of the [same] household of God" (v. 19). And in a slight shift of imagery, Paul pictures Jews and Gentiles not only sharing life in one family but actually becoming one holy temple (the Greek word *naos* suggests the inner shrine, the holy of holies where God's glory dwelt, Leviticus 16), inhabited by the most high God.

This access to God, this fellowship with him and all his people sums up the wonder of the gospel: no longer a distinction between those who were far and those who were near, between those who were Abraham's offspring and those who were not, between circumcised and uncircumcised. The Gentiles have become children of covenant, and the Jews trust the Messiah not the law for salvation. The barriers of the old Temple have been leveled. And one greater than Solomon has built a dwelling place for God from all who trust him and enter into the meaning of his peace.

GOSPEL: MARK 6:30–34

The early church often saw Jesus as a shepherd (John 10:11; 21:15–17; Heb. 13:20; 1 Pet. 5:4), revealing the loving care of the Lord (Ps. 23:1) and fulfilling the requirements of the true king (Jer. 23:1–6; Ezekiel 34). They recognized him in the parable of the shepherd who left the ninety-nine to search for the one lost sheep (Luke 15:3–7); they celebrated his remarkable care in the words of the elder of Revelation (7:17): "For the Lamb in the midst of the throne will be their shepherd."

Mark's account of Jesus' concern as shepherd in our lesson is illuminated by its context, following hard on the heels of the terrifying account of Herod's butchering of John the Baptist (6:14–29). If ever a king embodied all the traits that no good shepherd should have, it was Herod—savage in his use of power, profligate in his own moral life, extravagant in his wasteful opulence, scornful of his responsibility to do God's will as his regent.

The impact on the people was predictable: "They were like sheep without a shepherd" (v. 34), neglected at best and victimized at worst by those who should have led and tended them. Jesus' first response was *a feeling of compassion,* and that despite all the possibilities of other reactions: resentment at the intrusion of privacy, impatience spawned by fatigue and hunger (v. 31), preoccupation with the reports of the Twelve who had returned from their mission (v. 30). All that Jeremiah (23:1–6) had announced that shepherds should be in caring for their flocks and attending their needs, Jesus' compassion moved him to become.

But he demonstrated that compassion in a specific, surprising way: *a ministry of teaching* (v. 34). No healings are mentioned here, no demons called by name, no committees formed or plans of action devised. The needy multitude is ministered to at its point of deepest need—understanding the character of God, the nature of the kingdom, the good news of God's power and love released in their midst.

The thoughtful ones in that multitude may have heard in Jesus' teaching the fulfillment of Jeremiah's prophecy: "And I will give you a shepherd after my own heart, who will feed you with knowledge and understanding" (3:15). We would give a lot to know Jesus' curriculum. We can only guess from the accounts of his parables and instructions (e.g., Matthew 5—7; 13).

It is enough for us to know that Mark's picture of the shepherd-teacher is another sign that the true king was in Israel's midst. The scepter of the kingdom will one day be his, shaped like the shepherd's staff.

Mark's picture reminds us of the validity of our own ministries carried out in his name: "And his gifts were that some should be pastors [shepherds] and teachers" (Eph. 4:11). And Peter, whom Jesus himself had instructed in the care of God's precious sheep (John 21:15–17), passes that instruction on to us (1 Pet. 5:2–3). We shall tend the sheep better if we think of that busy day, that confused multitude, and that faithful shepherd who took time to teach.